# TOCQUEVILLE
# ON AMERICAN
# CHARACTER

# TOCQUEVILLE ON AMERICAN CHARACTER

WHY TOCQUEVILLE'S BRILLIANT
EXPLORATION OF THE AMERICAN SPIRIT
IS AS VITAL AND IMPORTANT TODAY AS IT WAS
NEARLY TWO HUNDRED YEARS AGO

## MICHAEL A. LEDEEN

TRUMAN TALLEY BOOKS
ST. MARTIN'S GRIFFIN
NEW YORK

www.stmartins.com

Library of Congress Cataloging-in-Publication Data

Ledeen, Michael Arthur.
Tocqueville on American character : why Tocqueville's brilliant exploration of the American spirit is as vital and important today as it was nearly two hundred years ago /
Michael A. Ledeen.
p. cm.
Includes bibliographical references and index.
ISBN 0-312-25231-5 (hc)
ISBN 0-312-28466-7 (pbk)
1. National characteristics, American. 2. United States—Civilization.
3. Tocqueville, Alexis de, 1805–1859—Political and social views. I. Title.
E169.1.L49 2000
973—dc21     00-029690

TRUMAN TALLEY BOOKS
First St. Martin's Griffin Edition: October 2001

10 9 8 7 6 5 4 3 2 1

# CONTENTS

# INTRODUCTION

———◆———

## RESTLESS PEOPLE INSPIRED BY IDEAS, FOREVER HEADED FOR NEW FRONTIERS

*The American dictionary is short in words of dignity, and names of honor.*
—CRÈVECOEUR

In the early summer of 1846, around a campfire at Fort Bernard on the North Platte River, several hundred settlers headed for Oregon and California met with a handful of the most famous explorers of the West moving in the opposite direction, eastward to the United States. The settlers had been lured to the Pacific Coast by promises of an earthly paradise, with land so fertile that crops burst spontaneously out of the earth, with climate so benevolent that merely living there would cure the diseases of those raised in the harsher East, and with natural beauty so intense that mere prose could not do it justice. As their inspirational guidebook, *The Emigrants' Guide to*

*Oregon and California* by Lansford W. Hastings, put it, "Here perpetual summer is in the midst of unceasing winter; perennial spring and never failing autumn stand side by side, and towering snow clad mountains forever look down upon eternal verdure."

It was not unusual for different generations of the westward expansion to meet on or beyond the frontier. When Lewis and Clark headed home barely a year after their discovery of the Northwest Passage, they encountered fur traders following their footsteps. These were the mountain men, who, while expanding American commerce, did the detailed exploration of the frontier. Lewis and Clark established that brave men could cross the continent, but the mountain men did the real micromapping. They were the ones who found the mountain passes through which the wagon trains ultimately traveled (Lewis and Clark moved over water, but the covered wagons didn't float), they were the ones who discovered which Indians were friendly, and which preferred to kill the white men. By 1846 there were enough rough roads through the deserts and mountains of the West to enable hucksters like Hastings to lure thousands of Americans (and European emigrants as well) to Oregon and California.

The settlers around the campfire that night were not the stuff of heroic legend, nor the tired and poor of later westward migration. Those destined for the greatest celebrity, the Donner family, were rich, and their wagons were the sports utility vehicles of their day: filled with gourmet foods, wines, and cognacs, and comfortable furniture and hi-tech stoves, drawn by the finest oxen and accompanied by the finest horses. The Donners were headed for California in search of comfort, not adventure. They were inspired by a dream of a better life for their children, not by desperation. The Donners owned lots of valuable land in Illinois, and they had plenty of money in hand: one of the quilts on board had ten thousand dollars in cash, a small fortune in those days, sewed into its chambers by the Donner women. Their traveling companions, the Reeds, had letters of introduction from leading politicians. James Frazier Reed was also no starving immigrant: the descendant of Polish aristocrats, born in Ireland, Reed was a successful farmer in Illinois.

The explorers around the campfire were not impressed with the settlers or with their handy guide to California. They had not read the Hastings book. They did not need to; one of their number, the legendary mountain man Jim Clyman, was one of the great explorers of the American frontier. Clyman and his colleagues in the fur trade had forged the trails that, by the mid-1830s, crisscrossed the deserts and mountains from the settled states of the American republic to the near-mythical territories of the West and northwest. The mountain men had discovered the "real" Northwest Passage, the land route by which wagon trains could cross the Continental Divide and make it safely to the coast. Clyman was truly the stuff of heroic legend, an American archetype.

. . . [T]his was an aggressive wilderness, its ferocity came out to meet you and the conditions of survival required a whole new technique . . . the mountain man must take to horse in a treeless country whose rivers were far apart and altogether unnavigable . . . the creek that dwindled in the alkali or the little spring bubbling for a yard or two where the sagebrush turned a brighter green was what your life hung on . . . one might go for days without sight of food, learn to live on rattlesnake or prairie dog, or when those failed on the bulbs of desert plants, or when they failed on the stewed gelatin of parfleche soles . . . Finally this was the country of the Plains Indians, horse Indians, nomads, buffalo hunters, the most skillful, the most relentless, and the most savage on the continent . . . Mountain craft was a technological adaptation to these hazards.[1]

Clyman despised Hastings, as any hero would loathe a con man, and Clyman knew from personal experience that Hastings was an utter fraud. Hastings had lured the settlers along a route neither he, nor anyone else had ever seen, let alone traveled. At the time he wrote *The Emigrants' Guide* Hastings had never seen the Humboldt River, or the Great Salt Lake, or the Wasatch Mountains, or the Salt Desert, all of which lay ahead of the Donners and the Reeds. Hastings had only just covered that territory, and in the opposite direction, traveling East with the best possible guide, Clyman himself. They had traveled on horseback, not with the burdensome wagons, and even so they found the route a hazardous one; without Clyman's experience and bravery Hastings might well have perished.

Clyman took great pains to tell the settlers that they must ignore Hastings' siren song and stick to the tried and true path—not the straight line on the map that Hastings had drawn, but a long and apparently cockeyed path that took them first south, then north, then south again. Clyman knew, probably better than any other living man, that the old route would probably get them across the desert and through the mountains before the winter snows arrived, while Hastings' directions would likely doom them. But these wealthy and comfortable travelers were not swayed from the alluring straight line on Hastings' map. Clyman kept a diary, and wrote down Reed's angry rejoinder: "There is a nigher route and it is no use to take so much of a roundabout course." Reed had it on good authority, *The Emigrants' Guide to Oregon and California*, page 137: "The most direct route . . . would be to leave the Oregon route, about two hundred miles east from Fort Hall; thence bearing west southwest to the Salt Lake; and then continuing down to the bay of San Francisco . . ."

The hell of it was that Reed and Clyman were old comrades-in-arms, having fought together in the Black Hawk War in Captain Early's backwoods fusiliers. Abraham Lincoln was another member of that illustrious group. Not even their early bonding in such a distinguished company could overcome the temptation of the easy road to paradise. It is as if the first settlers headed for the moon had dinner with their old friend Neil Armstrong, but instead of taking the advice of the man who had actually been there, preferred an overwritten book by a guy selling lots on the far side. But that's what they did.

The Donners and the Reeds went by the book, and it led them into a nightmare that has horrified Americans ever since. Battered by the extreme heat of the deserts, their wagons were broken in mud and fast-moving water, their herds were then depleted by lack of water and by relentless nighttime Indian raids. Undeterred, they doggedly followed Hastings' route, even when Hastings himself failed to appear as he had promised, and even though they saw, over and over again, that his estimates of travel time were wildly optimistic. In a triumph of blind hope over abundant empirical evidence, they stuck to Hastings' map.

The settlers organized themselves according to the rules of American democracy, electing their leaders and debating all the crucial decisions, but these noble habits were not designed to cope with the extreme threats that the frontier presented. The real wagon trains, as opposed to those Hollywood served up a century later, were rarely disciplined columns. Those who could, moved on quickly, leaving the stragglers to fend for themselves. Sometimes the advance parties sent back supplies and information, but often they did not.

As they dragged themselves toward their doom, the Donner party slowly went to pieces. Their household treasures (including a substantial library) were buried in the desert pending later retrieval, and their ability to work together was shattered. Fights broke out, friendships were destroyed, and the once-harmonious group divided and subdivided several times. Some of the party were smart enough to use mules instead of oxen, moved on ahead, and got through the mountains in time. Reed was attacked by one of the others, and killed him in self-defense. A makeshift jury found him guilty, and exiled him from the group, expecting him to die, but he was tougher and more resourceful than his would-be executioners. Reed caught up with the next contingent and arrived safely in California.

When the Donners entered the Sierras a terrible early snow was falling, and they were blocked in the Truckee River Valley by drifts that sometimes reached depths of twenty feet or more. Clyman's warnings had proven accurate.

Eighty-two people arrived at the Sierras with Donner, and only forty-seven made it through the ghastly ordeal of that winter. Some died in the camp at the edge of what is now called Donner Lake, others, including Reed (who had returned to try to rescue his family) perished in a valiant attempt to break through the terrible pass— Donner Pass of course—to bring back supplies and men capable of leading them to safety. Many died of starvation, and some of them were eaten by the survivors. Once the taboo was broken others were deliberately murdered to provide nourishment. It shocks us today, but it was hardly extraordinary in those times and places. No less an authority than Kit Carson warned anyone who would listen not to walk in front of his friend and colleague Bill Williams when the food ran out.

The Donner survivors ultimately arrived in California in piteous condition, but at least they were clothed. Jessy

Quinn Thornton, a hypochondriac who had gone west because he believed he suffered from asthma, overcame a similar ordeal, and arrived half-dead in Willamette Valley, Oregon, in mid-November, 1846. He was buck naked, having prudently traded his clothes for a horse. It proved no obstacle to a typically American success story; shortly thereafter he became superintendent of a religious school, and just four months after his spectacular arrival, was judge of the Oregon Supreme Court. Like Donner and Reed, Thornton was a well-educated man of means. He was a native Virginian, studied law in London, was a friend of Stephen Douglas, and exchanged letters with Horace Greeley.

All these, and tens of thousands more, went west, and while many were galvanized into action by the kind of sales pitch that lured the Donners to the Truckee Valley, and others were inspired by the politicians' demand that America fulfill her Manifest Destiny and conquer the rest of the continent, and still others—most notably the Mormons—went to establish a utopia, the point is that most all of them went because of a vision, to fulfill a dream. Jim Clyman, who was born in Virginia during the presidency of George Washington, and died in Napa Valley, California, eighty-nine years later, a man who had seen it all and done it all, understood the nature of Americans. After he wasted his breath on the Donner party, he continued East, and came across a new tombstone in the wilderness, where Reed had buried his aged mother-in-law. "This stone shews us," Clyman noted in his diary, "that all ages and all sects are found to undertake this long tedious and even dangerous journey for some unknown object never to be realized even by those the most fortunate. And why? because the human mind can never be satisfied never at rest always on the strech for something new some strange novelty."[2]

Clyman's terse description didn't begin to do justice to the amazing dynamism of the men and women who tamed and settled the American frontier. He lacked the vocabulary. The best account had been given a few years earlier, and in a foreign language at that. An unusually perceptive Frenchman wrote a perfect description of the courageous and inquisitive ambition that drove Americans from their comfortable homes and settled habits to risk their lives in the wilds of the West:

They had not been obliged by necessity to leave . . .
the social position they abandoned was one to be
regretted, and their means of subsistence were certain. Nor did they [make their dangerous journey]
to improve their situation or to increase their wealth;
it was a purely intellectual craving that called them
from the comforts of their former homes; and in

facing the inevitable sufferings of exile their object was the triumph of an ideal.[3]

The writer was Alexis Charles Henri Clerel de Tocqueville ("Tocqueville" will do for us), a young French aristocrat who visited the United States in the early 1830s and wrote the classic two-volume study of American democracy. No one ever understood us so well as Tocqueville, which is why every generation of Americans has felt obliged to come to grips with his remarkable insights into our character.

But Tocqueville isn't talking about the Donners or any of the other settlers headed West in mid-century; he's describing the Pilgrims who came to New England two hundred years before. He knows that American character had not fundamentally changed in two hundred years, any more than it has in the subsequent hundred and fifty: Americans were and are forever on the move, constantly in search of greater freedom, greater wealth, and greater happiness, all in the name of an idea.

Tocqueville discerned a pattern in human history: the relentless advance of equality. And America was at once its greatest fulfillment, and the precursor of further advances all over the world.

First there had been monarchy, and all paid homage to a sole ruler. This had been challenged by powerful aristocrats, who tore away from the monarch enough power to make themselves a dominant force: aristocracy. Then came the revolutions of the eighteenth century, notably in America and then in France, in the name of democracy. No one could dispute the pattern, and nobody could long resist the advance of equality. And in that ineluctable advance, Americans were the most radical and the most successful. Tocqueville was the first to recognize that America had been chosen by Providence to determine the destiny of half the globe, the half that cherishes liberty and the unbridled creativity that only free peoples can unleash. So if anyone wanted to see mankind's future, he had to come to the United States and immerse himself in it. Which was exactly what Tocqueville did.

Tocqueville's writings on America occupy a unique position on our national bookshelf. No author, before or since, has so provocatively challenged us with our own highest ideals, and simultaneously pointed to our most perilous shortcomings. No one has so clearly identified the political beliefs and national passions that set us apart from the rest of the world, or so deeply probed the tensions, paradoxes, contradictions, and anxieties that make Americans the most revolutionary people on earth.

All this was accomplished when he was quite young (Tocqueville was born in 1805, and the two volumes appeared in 1835 and 1840), and was based on a trip of a mere nine months in 1831. He and his close friend Gustave de Beaumont used their status as junior judges to wangle a grant from the French government, ostensibly to study the novelties of the American prison system. But this was a cover for their deeper purpose: to study American democracy itself. In nine frenetic months, they traveled all over the country, from the Canadian border to the Western frontier, which reached as far west as Memphis. They took boats up and down the Mississippi, and they visited the major cities from New Orleans to Boston. They were received with open arms by most everyone they wanted to meet, from President Andrew Jackson to former President John Quincy Adams, from Catholic priests to New York lawyers, from frontiersmen in the Ohio forests to the soon-to-be-legendary Sam Houston on a Mississippi riverboat (en route to Washington with his Indian followers in tow). They talked to slave owners (Beaumont wrote a novel about slavery in America) and businessmen, to journalists and school teachers; a good cross section of Americans, in short.

Tocqueville had few of the credentials we normally associate with great scholars. He was home-schooled by the local priest (his mother, traumatized by the executions of several members of her family during the French

Revolution, was not an active force in the upbringing of the three Tocqueville boys, and his father, a prefect, was often absent). There was little diversion on the family estate, so he read extensively in his father's abundant library. In time, he was sent to high school in Metz, where, unlike his two older brothers, he was a mediocre student. Later he went to Paris for a law degree. Nothing in his education gave any hint of his genius, although he always did well in rhetoric.

Like most of the great political thinkers, Tocqueville has the advantage of coming to his subject early in its life, when its special features are easier to recognize. But even so, he sees very deeply into our national soul, and he understands the really big thing: that America's uniqueness is not caused by the mere luck of geography—although our location is enormously important—or the genius of the Founders or the institutions of the political or legal system—although each plays its part in the American success story. Traveling around America, he finds a remarkable spiritual and intellectual coherence, no matter what the physical setting. An American in the wilderness is fundamentally the same as a big-city sophisticate, and both share a common identity with New England entrepreneurs and southern planters. That is because the frontiersmen and the settlers were not *products* of the wilderness, but civilized people who had come

West to dominate nature and reshape it according to their desires.

In early July, Tocqueville sails across Lake Erie to Detroit, and from there, posing as potential settlers, he and Beaumont enter the Michigan wilderness with a "public official charged with the sale of lands," Major John Biddle. They penetrate the wilderness on horseback, and see with their own eyes the Americans who cleared the land, built log cabins, and made a new life. Tocqueville gives a brief description of the cabin and its contents, noting the presence of books by Shakespeare and Milton in the midst of primitive furniture. But it is the people themselves that most impress Tocqueville:

> The angular muscles and long thin arms and legs make you recognize . . . the native of New England. This man was not born in the solitude where he dwells. . . . His first years were passed in the bosom of an intellectual and reasoning society. . . . But if his physical forces seem beneath his enterprise, in his face, lined by the cares of life, reigns an air of practical intelligence, of cold and persevering energy, which strikes one at once . . .

Alongside the frontiersman is his woman, for whom Tocqueville develops great admiration verging on awe.

The pioneer's wife, he writes, "has torn herself in one instant and without hope of returning from that innocent cradle of her youth . . . It's on the bare ground of the wilderness on which her nuptial couch was placed." She has borne her burdens with dignity and grace: "Want, suffering, and loneliness have affected her constitution but not bowed her courage."[4]

These Americans are quite different from anything Tocqueville's seen in Europe, different even from the English who could well claim paternity of the North Americans. They are driven people, for only those driven by great passions and great ambitions could conquer a continent and remake it in their own image. But is this unique to Americans? Is it not the same with all explorers and pioneers everywhere and always? Does this not come with the territory of the frontier?

To his amazement, he finds that it does not; no sooner does Tocqueville step outside the boundaries of the United States than he finds a different kind of man. He compares Americans and Canadians living just across the border from one another, and finds dramatic differences in their spirit: the Americans think of themselves as transients and are planning their next move. They live at some distance from one another, and their towns are bursting with movement and activity. The Canadians are putting down deep roots, their houses are closely packed, and life is much calmer than it is a mere few hundred yards to the south. Land and houses cost much more in Canada (indeed, about the same as they do in France), people have less money in their pockets, and opportunity is more limited.

These differences are obviously not due to the physical environment. There is no change in climate or landscape when you cross the border, but there is an enormous change in the character of the people. The same remarkable contrast exists on the southern front. The differences between Americans and Mexicans across the Texas or California borders can't be explained by physical variations between the two countries, yet there is a world of difference between the people.

Tocqueville is driven to a radical conclusion: the success of America is due to the Americans themselves. Canadians and Mexicans are building a stable society, but the Americans are forever pushing past existing frontiers, simultaneously destroying and advancing civilization, their own and that of their fathers. Tocqueville is flabbergasted to see successful people on the frontier, leaving civilization behind in order to create something newer and freer. With each move West, the Americans leave the Old World and its mores and institutions farther and farther behind, filtering out the old institutions, and, above all, the old habits of thinking.

We know exactly when and where Tocqueville starts to understand this revolutionary process. He first describes it in a letter to his brother Jules on the fourth of December, 1831, following a trip to Ohio, the most recently settled area on the western frontier. The Americans of the Mississippi Valley, he says, are creating a new society, "the most singular state of affairs that has doubtless existed under the sun." Then comes the epiphany:

A people absolutely without precedents, without traditions, without habits, without dominating ideas even, opening for itself without hesitation a new path in civil, political, and criminal legislation; never casting its eyes about to consult the wisdom of other peoples or the memory of the past; but cutting out its institutions, like its roads, in the midst of the forests which it has come to inhabit and where it is sure to encounter neither limits nor obstacles . . . [5]

This is an error of exuberance, of course; he knows well that Americans would always have moral, political, and philosophical roots in the Old World, especially England, and *Democracy in America* is more modulated on the matter of American exceptionalism. Nonetheless, Tocqueville's epiphany goes to the heart of who we are and what we are. He knows all about our European past and should know that Americans cannot discard their heritage by a supreme act of will and physical energy. However, we, who rarely study history (even our own), do think of ourselves this way. We believe we can re-make the world every day, and if we work really hard we can do it before sundown. In the deepest sense, he's got it right, seeing us from the inside.

Not that he is one of us. Don't think that Tocqueville wants to give up his aristocratic life and head for the frontier! He isn't cut out for that sort of life, not least because he's frail and is forever falling ill. The American frontier was far too challenging for him, and his letters and notebooks are full of moaning about the "infernal" roads he is compelled to travel in inferior carriages without the spring suspension system typical of good European ones. He loves the luxury of the steamboats, but is frustrated by the frequency with which they run aground (three times in a month, at one unlucky stretch).

He's a spoiled aristocrat, in short. When he writes *Democracy in America*, back on the family estate in France, he moves the cattle to the farthest corner of the property so that no "moo" will interrupt his concentration. He dreads

the thought of having to make his mark in open competition with everybody around him, even though he knows
it's a much fairer system than his own. But he is sadly
convinced that the world is going American, and therefore
he's doomed to live in some version of America. Under
the circumstances, he wants to do his best to ensure that
France takes our best qualities, and avoids the worst.

It took a foreigner to best understand us, partly because a foreigner can be more objective, having grown
up outside, and partly because we are too busy doing
other things. We are forever getting on with it. We are
a revolutionary people, driving ourselves to new frontiers
in every generation, constantly creating and constantly
destroying. It's not always pretty. We have high ideals,
but we can be as ruthless as any people, a point driven
home to Tocqueville when he ponders the sad fate of the
American Indians who had the misfortune of getting in
our way to the West.

In the heart of this society, so policed, so prudish,
so sententiously moral and virtuous, one encounters
a complete insensibility, a sort of cold and implac-
able egoism when it's a question of the American
indigenies. The inhabitants of the United States do
not hunt the Indians with hue and cry as did the
Spaniards in Mexico. But it's the same pitiless in-

stinct which animates the European race here as everywhere else.[6]

But, like everything else in America, these attitudes are swept up in the incredible tempo of change, and Tocqueville meets emerging leaders of the republic who hold very different opinions of the red man. Some of these encounters are so fortuitous that a cynical person would suspect they were staged. On a riverboat churning down the Mississippi toward New Orleans in December, 1831, Tocqueville discovers that two of his fellow passengers are famous frontiersmen: Davy Crockett and Sam Houston. There is no recorded conversation with Crockett (although other travelers filled his ears with snide remarks about the low quality of politicians from the new West), but Tocqueville went out of his way to talk to Houston, who, after a brief career as governor of Tennessee, had left his wife to join an Indian tribe (Tocqueville thinks it was the Creeks, but it was more likely the Cherokees), marry a squaw, and lead a delegation to President Jackson to improve the Indians' lot. When Tocqueville meets him, Houston is on the verge of greatness. Within a few years he will have gone to Texas, defeated Mexico's greatest general, Santa Anna, at the battle of San Jacinto, become president of the Republic of Texas, and brought it into the United States.

But on the riverboat, he's just another failed frontier politician with a sleazy reputation. Tocqueville eagerly interrogates him about the Indians:

Q. Does it seem to you that the Indians have great natural intelligence?

. . . . "Yes, I don't believe they yield to any human race on this point," he began. "However, I am also of the opinion that it would be the same for the negroes; the difference you notice between the Indian and the negro seems to me to result solely from the different educations they have received. The Indian is born free; he makes use of that liberty from his very first steps in life. He is his own master as soon as he is capable; the paternal authority is even almost unfelt. Surrounded by dangers, hounded by needs, able to count on nobody, his mind has to be constantly on the alert to find the means of warding off such dangers and of sustaining life. This forced necessity gives the Indian's intelligence a degree of development and a sharpness that are often admirable. The common negro was a slave before being born, without pleasures as without needs, useless to himself. The first notions that he receives from life show him that he is the property of someone else,

22

that the care of his own future is not his concern, and that the very use of thought is for himself essentially a gift of providence."[7]

Each generation takes us farther away from our origins, and each generation finds a way to test itself, to leave an indelible mark for others to challenge and overcome. We still think of ourselves in those generational terms. Tocqueville would not be surprised to hear talk of "Generation X," or the "Boomers"; he knows that fathers hope their sons will achieve more than they did themselves, and thus each generation is given its own identity. Those rare generations that fail, that give in to self-indulgence or other sins of omission, get shameful names like "the lost generation," a collective scarlet letter that brands them unworthy of the national mission.

There is a contemporary European gag which has it that "America is the first country to go from barbarism to decadence without ever passing through civilization," but Tocqueville knows that this is a bitter joke, told by people who envy American energy and creativity, and do not understand the endless American cycle of destroying the dead weight of the past and shaping the future. It began with the Pilgrims, and continued with the revolutionaries and the frontiersmen on through the imperial conquest of the continent and the Civil War. It became a global force in our century, and remains an integral part of our national DNA. Tocqueville's enraptured account of Americans creating a new world on the western frontier is at one with Tom Wolfe's description of the flight pilots who carried us into space.

> [T]he idea was to prove . . . that you were one of the elected and anointed ones who had the *right stuff* and could move higher and higher and even— ultimately, God willing, one day—that you might be able to join that special few at the very top, that elite who had the capacity to bring tears to men's eyes, the very Brotherhood of the Right Stuff itself.

Tocqueville knows that such a grandiose enterprise carries enormous risks. It is not possible for everyone to succeed, for, even in a society devoted to giving every citizen political and even social equality, God does not grant us all the same talent and Fortune does not smile equally upon us. Many will fall by the wayside. Worse still, those who do succeed, even those chosen few with the Right Stuff, run special risks. Hailed as the highest exemplars of the American Dream, they often fall prey to corruption, and drag countless others down with them. Tocqueville, one of the most thoughtful members of a corrupt European aristocracy, knows well that corruption can subvert our unique character, and thus the entire American enterprise. Looking into the future, he draws an ominously familiar picture of what a failed America might look like.

If you're one of those hypermodern souls who has been trained by the high priests of current intellectual fashion, you may well bridle at the very idea of national character. Nowadays our children are told that we should focus on the fractions—female Americans, African Americans, Native Americans, Dead White Male Americans, and so forth. All those hyphenated Americans might not add up to a whole, after all. Tocqueville is intensely aware of the enormous variations among Americans, and welcomes the emphasis on the ethnic, religious, and regional differences, but he insists that there is a basic core from which we all draw our national energy and our national vision.

No greater tribute can be paid to a man than to credit him with a great action he did not take, or a great saying he did not coin. By that high standard Tocqueville has been fulsomely praised. Among others Dwight Eisenhower, Bill Clinton, Colin Powell, Ross Perot, and Pat Buchanan, have credited Tocqueville with saying "America is great because she is good, and if America ever ceases to be good, she will cease to be great."

He never said it, and doesn't believe it. He knows we're much more complicated.

# CHAPTER 1

———◆———

# DYNAMIC PEOPLE DRIVEN BY INTERNAL CONFLICTS

*All the tensions of the world have been imported by the United States.*
— RAOUL ROMOLI-VENTURI

"Nothing struck me more forcibly," Tocqueville tells us right at the beginning of his great work, "than the general equality of condition among the people."[1]

If two Americans meet on the street, they treat one another as equals, regardless of differences in wealth, physical beauty or strength, or intellectual or artistic talent. Not that there are no differences; he's a practicing Catholic, and insists that we are differently endowed by God, and he is well aware that those differences will be recognized and either help us or hurt (and of course he knew all about black slavery). Nonetheless, he's amazed to discover that Americans value one another equally, deal with each other in the same way, and give everyone—all else being equal—the same opportunities. There's none of that bowing and scraping that goes on in the Old World, where a person is automatically assigned a certain status depending upon his parentage alone. Americans don't like that sort of thing. When Ben Franklin was sent to France they asked him for his title. He replied, "Mr.," insisting that no greater honorific could be given a man. Americans don't kneel to kings or queens; we salute men and women worthy of our respect.

We know that some men are more gifted than others, but we believe that all men are entitled to equal treatment. "The gifts of the intellect proceed directly from God, and man cannot prevent their unequal distribution" he reminds us, but "the means that Americans find for putting them to use are equal."[2] Equality of condition, not equality of endowment.

This passion for equality among Americans has, in Tocqueville's words, a "prodigious influence . . . it gives a peculiar direction to public opinion and a peculiar tenor to the laws; it imparts new maxims to the growing authorities and peculiar habits to the governed." And this prodigious influence doesn't stop with politics and law; it is the universal solvent of our lives, it affects everything and "modifies whatever it does not produce." Equality is "the fundamental fact" of American life, and

Tocqueville was certain it would eventually become the fundamental fact of life everywhere, the driving force of a global democratic revolution. And if you doubt his prescience, ask Mikhail Gorbachev.

No one is automatically entitled to high status or even respect because of birth. Respect has to be earned; it doesn't come merely because you have a famous name. And it isn't hard to discover how Americans decide who is top dog: whoever gets the most money wins the game. Equality of condition produces an endless turmoil in which each tries to distinguish himself from the others by outdoing them in the basic American competition for wealth. Americans are always trying to get rich or even richer, and they are constantly on the move. Like the Donners and the Reeds, Americans are ready to pack up and go when opportunity or challenge beckons. And even when they get rich, they still don't stop, because getting even richer is a constant challenge and a never-ending thrill. Business, not baseball, is the great American sport. "The desire of prosperity has become an ardent and restless passion . . . and it soon becomes a sort of game of chance, which they pursue for the emotions it excites as much as for the gain it procures."[3]

Many contemporary commentators think they see a growing materialism in American society, as if, in some more austere earlier time, we were more idealistic and less attracted to money and the things money buys. But there is no such age of innocence in our past; we've been after the golden ring from the very beginning. Tocqueville has it doubly right: it's part of our national DNA, and we're in it both for the money and for the thrill of winning the contest. The critics call it a rat race; the winners, and most Americans, love the competition and wouldn't have it any other way.

American tycoons give away a substantial amount of their fortune, even as they work long hours to keep the money pouring in. Andrew Carnegie was afraid that he might corrupt his children by leaving them lots of money, so he gave away almost all of it before the kids were ruined. Bill Gates and Michael Milken routinely give away billions (the Milken family funds dozens of activities from medical research to educational and religious undertakings) as do numerous Wall Street millionaires who don't want it publicized. They've got all the money they need, indeed they have so much they have to hire people to figure out how to give it away. But they work feverishly to make even more, because the game's the thing. Americans are like the troops Henry V surveyed on the eve of battle:

I see you stand like Greyhounds in the slips,
Straining upon the start. The game's afoot . . .

To win the game, you have to work, and Americans work harder and longer than anyone else in the modern world. "Everybody works," Tocqueville ruefully observes, "and work opens a way to everything; this has changed the point of honor quite around and has turned it against wealth."[4] He sadly remarks that there are plenty of Americans with enough money to be able to permit themselves a life of leisure, but "public opinion forbade it, too imperiously to be disobeyed." They work anyway, and join the general competition.

It's tough. It's not for everybody; even those raised in it sometimes find it too tough. Some try to change the rules. The Massachusetts Youth Soccer Association invented "nonresult-oriented competition" for kids ten and under, and is itching to extend it to 12-year-olds. "We're trying to take away that 'you've-gotta-win-the-trophy' feeling," the registrar of the association told the Associated Press in the summer of 1998.[5] The anonymous AP reporter called it "soccer without the kick," and one of the players remarked "It's dumb and stupid. It's fun to win." In the 1960s university students demanded an end to "the concept of failure" in their classwork, and even today there are schools and colleges that do not give grades, preferring personalized essays describing each student's progress. The Pojoaque Elementary School in Santa Fe, New Mexico, decided to abolish letter grades in 1997, and two years later there was a scheme to dilute the competition for college entry by reinterpreting SAT scores in accordance with, among other factors, how many electrical and electronic devices were in students' homes.

These may be noble efforts, but they're doomed so long as Americans remain American. As General George Patton says in the opening scene of his movie, "the American people hate a loser."

In this wide open competition, the society is constantly churned from top to bottom. A man can come from nowhere to become president of the nation or CEO of a great corporation of his own creation. Dreamers like Jefferson might muse about a "natural aristocracy" that could lead America to glory, but Tocqueville is no such dreamer. He sees that Americans, both within the society and on the continent, are surging up and sinking down. There is no enduring aristocracy, natural or otherwise; there's a frantic competition. Each generation creates its own leaders, and the son of yesterday's famous family is tomorrow's average Joe.

To be sure, the winners aren't always the best. Tocqueville gets a good look at American political leaders, from John Quincy Adams to Sam Houston, and is not only unimpressed, but, like us, is often depressed by the spectacle. He and Beaumont were underwhelmed by a conversation with President Andrew Jackson:

> General Jackson . . . is a man of violent temper and very moderate talents; nothing in his whole career ever proved him qualified to govern a free people; and, indeed, the majority of the enlightened classes of the Union has always opposed him. But he was raised to the Presidency, and has been maintained there, solely by the recollection of a victory which he gained . . . a victory which was, however, a very ordinary achievement and which could only be remembered in a country where battles are rare.[6]

Military victory has carried many American presidential candidates to the White House, from George Washington to Dwight Eisenhower, and probably would have enabled General Colin Powell to win the presidency. In our own day, the White House has become home to men whose credentials were more modest still: peanut farming (Jimmy Carter), movie acting (Ronald Reagan), Kansas City politics (Harry Truman), and wheeling-and-dealing in Arkansas (Bill Clinton) or California and Washington, D.C. (Richard Nixon). State and local leaders are often even less impressive.

Tocqueville observes that the most talented Americans rarely go into politics, because political power is limited by an elaborate network of checks and balances that frustrates ambition and imagination. "I was surprised to find so much distinguished talent among the citizens and so little among the heads of the government,"[7] he muses, but it makes perfect sense. Business is far more challenging, more remunerative, and places fewer restrictions on the top people. Most CEOs have more power than most government officials, they get better perks, and they have higher prestige in society. No wonder that our best and brightest are more easily found in board rooms than in legislative chambers or executive branch offices. Would you rather be Warren Buffett or Bill Clinton? Do you think it's better to run American Airlines or be secretary of the air force? Do you think there's a higher talent level in the House of Representatives or in the top corporate boardrooms?

Tocqueville dryly remarks that it sometimes appears that you have to fail in business in order to undertake a career in politics. The business successes aren't often tempted to run for high office, and when they do, they usually lose prestige. Ask Ross Perot, Steve Forbes, or Donald Trump.

As Tocqueville found, America is wide open. There is no other country in which almost any child can legitimately dream of becoming . . . anything. No other people find it perfectly normal when a college dropout named Bill Gates becomes the richest man in the world virtually overnight, or when an immigrant named Kwok Li sells his eight-year-old company to Lucent Technologies for a billion dollars in cash, when immigrants named Henry Kissinger and Madeleine Albright are entrusted with the foreign policy of the United States, or a member of the Georgian black underclass named Clarence Thomas becomes a Supreme Court justice. Seventy percent of our current millionaires achieved their status during their lifetimes. Americans, Tocqueville concludes, "are there seen on a greater equality in point of fortune and intellect, or, in other words, more equal in their strength, than [are people] in any other country of the world, or in any age of which history has preserved the remembrance."[8]

This is the "equality of condition" that so impresses Tocqueville. While wealth is indeed unevenly divided at any given moment, there are no permanent classes. From time to time there are anguished cries about a growing gap between rich and poor in America, as if this were terribly unfair, particularly when a small percentage of the population makes enormous sums of money. But Americans themselves, including those at the bottom of the pile, don't agree with the critics. Americans overwhelmingly believe that equality of condition exists, and that they can benefit from it. Two-thirds of Americans polled in 1993 (just after a brief economic recession) answered "yes" to the question, "do you think people should be allowed to accumulate as much wealth as they can even if some make millions while others live in poverty?"[9] Three years later, an astounding 80 percent agreed that it is possible to "start out poor, work hard, and become rich." This conviction spans social categories and ethnic groups, from top to bottom. When *The Washington Post* asked African American teenagers in 1995 whether blacks or whites had a better chance to succeed in life, 60 percent said the chances were equal.[10]

To be sure, as in George Orwell's memorable phrase, some people are more equal than others. Rockefellers and Kennedys, and now Buffetts and Gateses, have more opportunity than people born at the bottom of the feeding chain. There are many people who, through no fault of their own, are not going to succeed. Tocqueville knows this, but he also knows that the chances for success are greater here than anywhere else, and that our belief in our unique opportunities drives us, in a powerful self-fulfilling prophecy, to break down barriers to social mobility.

For Tocqueville, the most revolutionary thing about America is the constant dynamic change up and down the social ramp: poor people get rich, and rich guys become impoverished. This means that categories such as "rich" and "poor" contain constantly changing faces; America is not divided into fixed classes the same way as other societies. In the Old World, with rare exceptions that prove the general rule, political power is retained and transmitted by political parties or family dynasties, and wealth either flows from the coffers of the state or is passed on from wealthy parents to their fortunate children. That is why young and ambitious Europeans and Asians, brandishing their new MBAs or certificates of proficiency in computer programming, or acceptance letters from American universities, are headed for the United States in record numbers. At last count there were more than half a million foreign students in our colleges and universities, with the numbers growing every year.

In the rest of the world, those who are born in the wrong neighborhood learn early on that they're not destined for wealth or glory. In England or Italy, the wrong accent can close most of Fortune's doors. If non-Americans want to move up, they must generally choose among the traditional channels of limited upward mobility: the church, the military, or organized crime. Most Americans, whatever their origins, think they can become millionaires and live the good life. A recent book title, of which hundreds of similar examples can easily be found, proclaims: *Getting Rich in America: Eight Simple Rules for Building a Fortune and a Satisfying Life.* Luigi Barzini, another keen-eyed European visitor to America, mused on this uniquely American phenomenon almost exactly a century after Tocqueville's trip.

> Only the fools, the lazy, the inept, the irresponsible, and the egotists refused to face the challenge. They had no excuse. Cheap handbooks, as simple to follow as cookbooks for new brides, taught everybody in simple language how to develop their dormant talents and the tricks necessary to make a packet quickly, possibly in their youth, in order to spend the rest of their life fishing. One could learn for a few dollars how to speak masterfully in public, be irresistible, dominate a meeting, mesmerize superiors or opponents, make friends, sell everything to everybody, and, in the end, with the first million in the bank, spot prodigious investment opportunities, investments that multiplied themselves like amoebas . . . People hopefully bought these books by the millions, as true believers buy sacred relics or bottles of miraculous water at a sanctuary.[11]

Sometimes Americans become millionaires without even trying. A young employee of America Online, hired to put data into the on-line sports reports, had accumulated a bundle of AOL stock options without knowing their significance. One happy day in the summer of 1999 a colleague told him that the shares were now "vested," and were worth more than two million dollars. It was better than winning the lottery, even though it was hardly won by merit. Sometimes you just get lucky.

But the basic rule is that if you work hard, you'll make it. To quote Ron Jones, the co-owner of Handy Andy Janitorial Services in Plano, Texas: "If you want your prayers answered, get off your knees and hustle."[12] And Marcus Garvey, the celebrated black leader of the early twentieth century, said it all: "Wealth is power, wealth is justice, wealth is real human rights . . . The opportunity is yours, you can lift yourselves to any height . . ."[13]

That is why our greatest heroes do it on their own. "There is a new glorification of the risk-taking businessman," *The Wall Street Journal* tells us in its "Overview of World Business" in late 1999. "According to one recent survey, more than 90% of Americans consider the entrepreneur a figure of respect . . . In the U.K. . . . the figure was just 38%. And in Japan, only 8% of adults believe it is prestigious to start a company."[14]

Tocqueville knows how avidly we glorify risk-taking pioneers. Today, Jim Clyman would be an Internet ty-

coon or an astronaut. Those 1999 poll results were just
another reflection of one of the basic components of
American character. The lone figure challenging the
frontier—whether the actual wilderness of our first two
hundred and fifty years; or the frontiers of industry,
sports, and space; or the frontiers of the mind—is the
quintessential American hero. We have always been
moving west, and when the real west became too civilized we moved on to conquer other worlds.

He chooses his words carefully: We were conquerors
long before the world wars of the twentieth century. You
have only to look, as Tocqueville does, at the fate of the
Indian tribes that fell before our western march. He describes us in terms that conjure up visions of Roman
legions:

> ... a restless, reasoning, adventurous race which
> does coldly what only the ardour of passion can
> explain ... nation of conquerors who submit them-
> selves to the savage life without ever allowing
> themselves to be seduced by it ... A people which,
> like all great peoples, has but one thought, and
> which is advancing toward the acquisition of riches,
> sole goal of its efforts, with a perseverance and a
> scorn for life that one might call heroic, if that name
> fitted other than virtuous things.[15]

Shades of Jim Clyman's meditation at the gravesite of Reed's mother! If the legendary mountain man—the exemplar of Tocqueville's description—had had Tocqueville's gift of language, and the time to think it through, he'd have said the same.

All we ask for is a level playing field. Give us a fair chance, don't give the other guys any advantage, and we think we'll make it. That is why that most un-American practice, the quota system of favoring one group over another, is cut down time after time, whether it is applied to Catholics, Jews, Blacks, Latinos, or women. We do not wish to give or receive special treatment.

In our rough-and-tumble society, there are no guarantees. Equality cuts both ways. You can rise from squalor to Beverly Hills, and you can fall from the heights of Wall Street and take your place amidst the Bowery bums. Nobody bats an eye when yesterday's tycoon slides down into the yaw of the struggling masses. It can happen to the greatest of us, even to Superman's wife. Margot Kidder, who played Lois Lane in the movie version of the superhero's life, was found wandering the streets of southern California, her fortune spent, her clothes in tatters, and her mind befuddled. Joe Lewis, the great heavyweight boxing champion, was reduced to penury, as are countless former stars of professional sports. Once they were among the richest of us.

41

We know that the bigger they are, the harder they fall. It's all part of the American game, an almost daily occurrence. The Dart Group, once a booming empire that owned major interests in Dart Drug Stores, Crown Books, Trak Auto, Total Beverage, and Shoppers Food Warehouse, was torn apart by generational conflict, which not only paralyzed the enterprise but generated enormous legal costs as father and sons sued and countersued each other. Boston Chicken, one of the hottest new stocks in the country in 1993, filed for bankruptcy barely five years later. Woolworth, the very symbol of the American department store, has vanished, along with former business giants like Eastern and Western Airlines. Pan Am used to be the greatest airline in the world; today it is a regional shadow of its former glory.

We may mourn their passing, but we welcome the opportunity to rise to their former heights, and then surpass them.

## The Perfectibility of Man

When an entire people demonstrates a unique passion for achievement, they must be motivated by some basic cause, such as an underlying belief, a blessing of fortune, a powerful new development, or perhaps a profound internal conflict. If it were just a matter of a lucky location on good land with nonthreatening neighbors, then the Canadians and the Mexicans would be just like us. If it were just a matter of our British heritage, we'd be just like the Australians. Tocqueville has met ambitious individuals before, and he knows that ambition is a basic human trait. But this is something quite different from the usual man-on-the-make: he's found an entire people racing full speed ahead, and we've kept on racing for more than three hundred years.

Tocqueville lays it at the altar of Equality. In traditional societies, where a man's status is determined at birth, individuals can improve themselves but it is inconceivable to improve everyone. That would undo the entire social fabric. In America, where all are deemed equal, where no one is fixed in place, and where you can go from the bottom to the top in a single lifetime, everyone can improve, or be improved.

It also means that nothing is forever; if we're going to make everything, and everybody better, the old models have to be thrown away. We call it "creative destruction," and it was part and parcel of the American character long before it became a slogan for business visionaries like "Neutron Jack" Welsh of General Electric, who has created more shareholder wealth than any chief executive in history, and earned his nickname by firing nearly a quarter of his employees: ". . . the radical messages he began preaching 20 years ago now seem like clichés . . . Conference speakers the world over assert that you have to destroy your own business to survive."[16]   Creative destruction has always been a fundamental component of our DNA, because we have always been perfecting our enterprises . . . and ourselves. No one knows it better than Welsh, who, according to *Business Week* magazine, has a "near spiritual belief in the promise of the individual." Welsh could have been quoting Tocqueville when he said "The idea flow from the human spirit is absolutely unlimited . . . All you have to do is tap into that well. I don't like to use the word efficiency. It's creativity. It's a belief that every person counts."[17]

The belief in the perfectibility of mankind was an Enlightenment conceit, but in Europe it was embraced by a mere handful of philosophers (the ones famously spoofed by Voltaire in *Candide*). Over here it became an article of national faith. Americans hold a truly revolutionary, even messianic belief in the perfectibility of mankind. Tocqueville looks deeply into the American soul, and finds, in the midst of our frenetic activity,

[T]he image of an ideal but always fugitive perfection . . . Continual changes are then every instant occurring . . . the position of some is rendered worse, and he learns but too well that no people and no individual, however enlightened they may be, can lay claim to infallibility; the condition of others is improved, whence he infers that man is endowed with an indefinite faculty for improvement. His reverses teach him that none have discovered absolute good; his success stimulates him to the never-ending pursuit of it. Thus, forever seeking, forever falling to rise again, often disappointed, but not discouraged, he tends unceasingly towards that unmeasured greatness so indistinctly visible at the end of the long track which humanity has yet to tread.[18]

That madcap pursuit of happiness for all men, one of those basic human rights that Jefferson laid down in the Declaration of Independence, isn't an abstract philosophical ideal; it's our core principle. It infuses our every activity, from physical workouts designed to give us perfect bodies, to varieties of religious and mystical experience that promise us perfect souls, and scientific research that promises triumph over disease, birth defects, and perhaps even death itself. We believe that we all have "an indefinite faculty for improvement."

Tocqueville's compact description of our outlook on life is deadly accurate. Americans consider failure temporary; what matters, as our mothers taught us, is how much you learn from it, and whether or not you grow stronger thereafter. Thomas Alva Edison had over six thousand failed attempts to find the right filament for his electric light bulb, and he proudly insisted that he learned something each time. We love comebacks, whether by a team that falls behind in the first half or by a defeated man who tries again and again until he finally wins. Sylvester Stallone's "Rocky," an archetypal American hero, never has an easy fight. He always gets bashed in the early rounds, and has to pick himself up from the mat, and come back to win.

As so often in American life, there is a religious underpinning to our fundamental optimism. Americans love repentant sinners, the moral equivalents of losers who find the wherewithal to come back and win. No wonder Bill Clinton's most affectionate nickname is "the Comeback Kid." Consider also the spectacle of the "Ninth 1st Annual IG Nobel Prize" ceremony in Cambridge Massachusetts, honoring achievements that "cannot or should not be reproduced." As awards were bestowed on such breakthrough creations as "a device to aid women giving birth: a circular table that rotates at high speed," and a study of why cereal gets soggy, a live Internet feed was managed by one Robert T. Morris.

Morris teaches computer science at the Massachusetts Institute of Technology, is an Internet million-
aire, and serves on the . . . editorial board. He's also
a convicted felon who was sentenced to community
service and three years' probation by a federal judge
after a computer "worm" program he wrote clogged
operating systems around the world and brought
much of the Internet to its knees in 1989. The *New
York Times* called it "the largest assault ever on
America's computers." He has since earned a doc-
torate in computer science from Harvard, and an
estimated $9 million from the sale of an Internet
start-up company he co-founded."[19]

Even convicted felons can make it in America, provided they repent and start anew on the road to perfection.

Human perfectibility is one of the most radical ideas
in human history, and a society that embraces it is both
revolutionary and intensely frustrated. America is a truly
revolutionary society, and ours is the one successful revolution in modern history, as Tocqueville repeatedly reminds us. The French Revolution produced massive
bloodshed, a world war, and then failure. The Russian
Revolution produced bloodshed, then organized terror

for three quarters of a century, then failure. The fascist revolutions in Italy and Germany produced a world war, the Holocaust, and then humiliating defeat. The Chinese Revolution killed more people than all the others combined, and China is still looking for a workable solution to its enormous problems. The American Revolution produced a great success, and we are still succeeding more than two centuries later.

As Tocqueville foresaw, America is a global revolutionary force, threatening tyrants everywhere, as their subjects learn that the most successful country in the world is also the freest. The citizens of the old Soviet Empire knew all along that they'd be better off living in a free society than under communist dictatorship, and they knew that America was the best model of what they wanted. But Americans are frustrated because, despite all our best efforts, we never quite get there.

Sometimes we even lapse back into nostalgia for the (generally imaginary) good old days when men were born to a position, and just stayed there. Examples range from the charming to the pathetic, as American adults play dress-up and pretend to be aristocrats. There is a current boomlet in formal shooting clubs, whose members

come out of their closets monthly in tweed jackets, waistcoats, breeches, stockings, knee flashes and other sartorial accessories of turn-of-the-century lords. Along with their ladies (usually wives) in ankle-length skirts, fluffy high-neck blouses and feathered hats, they gather to ape the elegance, lavishness and style of English shooting parties in their vintage years from 1880 to the beginning of World War I.[20]

One of the members, the security chief of a watch company in New York, goes right to the heart of the matter: "We want to Americanize the whole concept of elitism." It's a cozy refuge from the endless ordeal of perfecting mankind.

On the other hand, we're sure we will get there, once we find the right combination of leaders and laws. And we're also sure that we're making constant progress. We are better off than our parents, and our children will do better than we have. Step by glorious step, we're moving forward. Things are getting better all the time, and if they're not, we'll fix it.

That is why Americans invented the concept of planned obsolescence, which takes for granted that today's technological breakthrough will be tomorrow's collector's item, just as the first big computer, the Univac, is now a museum piece. Tocqueville greatly admired American know-how, and was quite taken with the elegant design of our sailing ships, but he could not refrain from commenting to an American ship builder that the materials weren't as durable as those used in European ships. The American immediately agreed, and gave a typically American explanation: Why should we use the best materials when we know that the next generation of ships will be even better, and in just a few years we will want to use the newer models? Ralph Nader was furious when he discovered that American automobile manufacturers still used the same strategy a century and a half later. If he'd read Tocqueville more carefully, he'd have understood that it's a logical consequence of our belief that everything and everyone can and will be made better and better.

Nonetheless, life remains stubbornly imperfect and inequalities continue to abound, even in the midst of American abundance. Barzini recognizes that this is the stuff of the ancient Greek myth of Sisyphus, doomed to push a rock up a steep mountain, but never reaching the summit. Whenever he gets near the peak, the rock eludes him and rolls back to the bottom. It is a metaphor for the endless pursuit of the American dream.

Americans, men engaged in their unending Sisyphean labor without rest . . . had always been tormented by the perennial discovery that their achievements were always late and inferior to the dream, that every gain had to be paid for with heartbreaking and irremediable losses. From the beginning their expectations had always been so high that the results, no matter how spectacular, were bound to be disappointing. Impatience and a feeling of frustration were the two faces of America.[21]

Tocqueville's exploration of American character has uncovered a basic tension: We believe in the perfectibility of man, but we are clear-eyed enough to recognize our failures. We know that the fault, as Shakespeare put it, lies not with our stars but with ourselves, and each failed generation leaves its successor with a heavier messianic burden.

This is the kind of psychological conflict that explains our frenetic nature, and Tocqueville knows that it is only one of many.

It doesn't bother us, mind you; but it does drive us to try even harder. It's what makes us so dynamic. It's why we, with 5 percent of the world's population, generate half of the world's venture capital. We intend to build that glorious "city on the hill" of which John Winthrop spoke in Puritan Massachusetts.

Maybe the game's not the main thing. Maybe the stakes are higher.

## A Tortured and Revolutionary People

By the time Tocqueville meets us, we've been through a lot: the original immigration and the first harsh years in the New England woods and the disease-ridden Chesapeake Bay, then several wars, first with the Indians and then with the French, and of course the long Revolutionary War with the English. The tough century and a half between the arrival of the Pilgrims and the defeat of the British army weeded out those who weren't up to the challenge, or who simply wanted a less stressful life. Sometimes it was voluntary: people did go back to the Old Country, and others migrated to Canada, where the crown still held sway. On other occasions it was a forced emigration, or a choice made under desperate circumstances. The American Revolution produced a far higher percentage of émigrés than the French Revolution— something approaching 100,000 royalists out of the 2.5 million living here at the time—and, with exceptions so rare they can be counted on the fingers of one mutilated hand, they never came back. After the French Revolution, the royalists returned and restored the monarchy, but not in America. Our royalist émigrés gave quaint and wistful names to tiny towns and villages on the Bahamian islands where they settled (and where their descendants still live), awaiting the defeat of the revolutionaries and the restoration of British rule: Hope, Patience, and so forth.

Those who went to Canada remained tied to the Old World and its mores, as Tocqueville neatly shows us in his comparison between the two towns on different sides of the border. They are still inclined to follow the European lead, rather than, as we prefer, to thumb our noses at foreign methods. Nearly a quarter-century ago, the United States and Canada agreed to adopt the metric system. Both countries decided to move in unison. In order to avoid confusion, joint labeling was introduced years in advance: liquid containers were marked in quarts, gallons and liters, while items on grocery store shelves were weighed in pounds, ounces, grams, and kilos. When the appointed day arrived, Canada saluted briskly and switched over. In America . . . nothing happened. The Canadians now use kilometers, kilograms, and the centigrade scale; we stuck with miles, gallons, and Fahrenheit. Americans just weren't interested in conforming to international practice.[22]

The great historian of the Revolutionary period, R. R. Palmer, concluded that our national consensus, which is to say our national character, "rests in some degree on the elimination from the national consciousness, as well as from the country, of a once important and relatively numerous element of dissent."[23]

The royalists are gone; the revolutionaries are us.

This rigorous selection process left us with a clear and unique national character, but, as Tocqueville quietly admits in his less effervescent moments, certainly not a monolithic one. Had the entire country been subjected to the harsh rigors of New England Puritanism, it might have been too constricting. Had the country instead adopted the more self-indulgent and aristocratic style of the Chesapeake Bay Colony—morality was more lax in the South from the very beginning—it might have excessively diluted our national Calvinist ethic.

For one thing, our passion for equality is closely linked to two other components: freedom and *individualism* (a word coined by Tocqueville). Most Americans think that freedom and equality are essentially the same thing, or two sides of the same coin: We think that freedom and equality have been granted to each individual, in order that he can pursue happiness and success as he sees fit.

But most Americans are wrong. In one of the darkest

sections of *Democracy in America*,[24] Tocqueville erects a temporary firewall between freedom and equality, a second tension in the American character. "A man may be the equal of all his countrymen save one, who is the master of all . . ." In a dictatorship, everyone except the ruler is equal, but none but the dictator is free. And although we can't be absolutely equal unless we're entirely free, "the taste which men have for liberty and that which they feel for equality are, in fact, two different things; and . . . among democratic nations they are two unequal things." Americans are more passionately devoted to the pursuit of happiness—to be sure, happiness pursued by equally free individuals—than to defending liberty, even though you can't achieve ultimate happiness without maximum freedom. Tocqueville will drag us back to that thought again and again. Good aristocrat that he is, he values liberty more than equality, and he's afraid that, in our headlong and sometimes unreasoned embrace of equality, we may someday lose our freedom.

"Freedom" also turns out to be more complicated than you might imagine. As David Hackett Fischer has painstakingly recounted,[25] there were four variations on the theme, as one would have expected, from four distinct groups of immigrants, from four English regions during the seventeenth century. All came in search of greater freedom, but there were differences, sometimes substantial ones, which the settlers brought with them.

- New England developed an "ordered freedom," stressing obligation and discipline in a strict religious context;
- Virginia translated the aristocratic traditions of its founder into a "hegemonic freedom," and stressed notions of collective honor and dignity (in a direct line to Jefferson's natural aristocracy);
- The Pennsylvania Quakers insisted on "reciprocal freedom" verging on modern libertarianism;
- The back country frontiersmen were advocates of "natural freedom," and produced the lion's share of the great explorers and mountain men, from Daniel Boone forward.

While our four versions of freedom varied from region to region (as they do even today), they blended into an American consensus. "This diversity of libertarian ideas," Fischer reminds us, "has created a culture of freedom which is more open and expansive than any unitary tradition alone could possibly be."

So there is turmoil even over this, our political and

social bedrock. We are committed to freedom, like no people before us, but we are not united in our understanding of exactly what freedom means, or what a free society should be like. On occasion we've had some very nasty ruckuses about freedom. We fought the bloody Civil War over whether or not the Southern states could freely secede from a union into which they had freely entered. Earlier, we argued furiously over how to organize a constitution for a free country. Our contemporary political debates are models of tranquility compared to those arguments in Philadelphia, let alone to the battlefields of the 1860s.

The American ferment is not limited to competition among us; it goes on within us as well. A people constantly on the move is not tranquil, and our constant motion bespeaks an intense inner turmoil. Tocqueville spots it right away, and he marvels that it is not the result of the desperation of the poor, or even the zealousness of those on the make, but a basic component of the American character, leading him to suspect that there is a higher rate of insanity in America than in the Old World. He finds an unexpected tension even within the souls of the most successful. Tocqueville marvels that while he has encountered "the freest and most enlightened men placed in the happiest circumstances that the world affords; it seemed to me as if a cloud habitually hung upon their brow, and I thought them serious and almost sad, even in their pleasures." The constant quest for unlimited happiness and unending success obsesses Americans, driving them in a near frenzy toward ever-greater accomplishments: ". . . It is strange to see with what feverish ardor the Americans pursue their own welfare, and to watch the vague dread that constantly torments them lest they should not have chosen the shortest path which may lead to it . . ."[26] Two centuries later, Barzini remarked upon the same phenomenon:

> Most unhappy of all . . . were many successful people, who should theoretically have been the happiest, because every one of them thought he had not really gone as far as he deserved, and felt cheated, or because, with success, his new problems had multiplied and become unendurable.[27]

Our belief in individualism creates a third tension, because the American enterprise is also collective. We are all striving to build that city on the hill, and we hope and expect that our individual efforts will eventually bring freedom and happiness to everyone. Ralph Barton Perry, following in Tocqueville's footsteps, has called this particular tension a collective individualism:

American self-reliance is a plural, collective, self-reliance—not "*I* can," but "*we* can." But it is still individualistic—a togetherness of several and not the isolation of one, or the absorption of all into a higher unity. The appropriate term is not "organism" but "organization"; ad hoc organization, extemporized to meet emergencies, and multiple organization in which the same individuals join many and surrender themselves to none.[28]

A collective individualism was precisely what the Donners and the Reeds exemplified, but their example shows the perils of a society that admires the individual above all else (which is why Tocqueville believed individualism to be a vice). There are tasks that can only be accomplished if individuals forget their personal interests and sacrifice for the group or community or nation. And there are times when all the individuals will be wiped out unless the group cohesion holds. Marine trainees are not permitted to use the word "I," because they must submerge their egos in the interests of the mission. Marine drill sergeants dread the breakdown of the group, because once soldiers start thinking about their personal interests, they will not fight effectively. The military is the extreme example of the desperate need for collective enterprise, but it is far from the only one; even before the terrible snows in the Truckee Valley, the Donner Party had broken under the strain of the long trek across the continent.

The Donners did not lose their individualism. They lost their lives.

American individualism begins in the cradle. American parents deliberately set out to raise young men and women who will think for themselves, and grow up to be successful individuals. And it works: 69 percent of Americans polled in 1989 agreed that "it is boring to live like other people," compared, for example, with only a quarter of Japanese. We love daring individuals, and our heroes do not blend in with the crowd. We hail the Lone Ranger and Superman, and we do not like it when they are tamed. When Superman proposed to Lois Lane in *Superman II*, a groan went through a New York City audience, and one spectator screamed, "Don't do it Supe!" Luke Skywalker has to fight Darth Vader by himself; not even his gurus can help him. Rambo has to fight the elite forces of the Red Army virtually alone, and Tom Clancy's CIA hero fights by himself, against bad guys at home and abroad. When Ronald Reagan taunted his political enemies by quoting Dirty Harry's immortal words: "Go ahead. Make my day," he knew what he was doing.

## THE TYRANNY OF THE MAJORITY

The most fundamental and the most dangerous of these internal tensions is the "collective" part of "collective individualism." The French philosopher Jacques Maritain described it as a perpetually varying tension "between the sense of the community and the sense of individual freedom."[29] It's a creative tension, so long as there is a reasonable balance between the two. But we have a tendency to go overboard, either toward anarchy or what Tocqueville ominously calls the "tyranny of the majority."

This dark side of American character is the product of democracy itself, which places the government under the sovereignty of the people, expressed in the election of our representatives. Tocqueville fears that the power of the majority will squash our individualism, blunt our creativity, and produce a mindless conformity throughout our society. He compares the power of the American majority with that of the absolute monarchs of Europe:

The French . . . held it for a maxim that the king could do no wrong; and if he did do wrong, the blame was imputed to his advisers. This notion made obedience very easy; it enabled the subject to complain of the law without ceasing to love and honor the lawgiver. The Americans entertain the same opinion with respect to the majority.[30]

We may not hold our individual fellow citizens in great esteem, but we adulate them when they express themselves collectively, believing with the ancient Romans that "the voice of the people is the voice of God." Tocqueville is not surprised (even though he is deeply disappointed) when politicians make important decisions on the basis of public opinion polls, muttering that "with the exception of the tumult, this comes to the same thing as if the majority itself held its deliberations in the market-place." He much prefers leaders who present their own ideas, reach their own conclusions, and then invite their electors to evaluate the results.

Since we think the desires of the majority are superior to those of any minority, there is always the risk that minorities will be trampled, even in the normal course of day-to-day life. In an excess of anxiety, Tocqueville goes so far as to despair of any true freedom of expression. "I know of no country in which there is so little independence of mind and real freedom of discussion as in America . . . there is but one authority, one element of strength and success, with nothing beyond it."[31] An oppressive conformity, in other words, that denies to a maverick thinker the courtesy of an open hearing.

Tocqueville paints a nightmare vision of what happens to someone who sets himself against the conventional American wisdom. Such a man, he says, can say or write whatever he wishes, but he will be scorned. "Every sort of compensation, even . . . celebrity, is refused to him." He is abandoned by all, even those who used to encourage him.

"He yields at length, overcome by the daily effort he has to make, and subsides into silence, as if he felt remorse for having spoken the truth." Tocqueville considers this worse than the oppressive censorship of the absolute monarchies, in which "the body was attacked in order to subdue the soul; but the soul escaped the blows . . . and rose proudly superior." Under the democratic tyranny he sees rising in America, the body is left intact, but the mind and the soul are suffocated.

The [democratic master] says: "You are free to think differently from me and to retain your life, your property, and all that you possess; but you are henceforth a stranger among your people. You may retain your civil rights, but they will be useless to you, for you will never be chosen by your fellow citizens if you solicit their votes; and they will affect to scorn you if you ask for their esteem. . . . Your fellow creatures will shun you like an impure being . . . Go in peace! I have given you your life, but it is an existence worse than death."[32]

Our belief in the wisdom of the majority leads to contempt for the politically incorrect, whatever the current version of political correctness, because our faith in public opinion is a kind of civic religion, "and the majority its ministering prophet."[33] That is why our leaders wrap themselves in the mantle of "the people," and even if they advance unpopular ideas they claim the support of a "silent majority." Tocqueville fears that our worship of the collective wisdom of the American people may one day replace the old forms of oppression with a new one, and he issues a stern warning: "When I feel the hand of power lie heavy on my brow, I care but little to know who oppresses me; and I am not the more disposed to pass beneath the yoke because it is held out to me by the arms of a million men."[34]

Tocqueville foresees a terrible leveling of talent, from politics to science, art and literature, all due to the tyranny of the majority. Forgetting his earlier insight that the most talented people will stay out of politics, he intones that the mediocre quality of American leaders is due to the despotism of the majority. In like manner, since he sees no great writers in America, he blames it on the usual suspect: "There can be no literary genius without freedom of opinion, and freedom of opinion does not exist in America."

He is certainly right about our touching faith in the wisdom of the majority, and he is at least half-right about our proclivity to impose group standards on individuals who try to swim against the mainstream. We have gone through many moments when it appeared that Tocqueville's nightmare was on the verge of establishing the rules of daily life. Those of us who grew up in the 1950s and grimly read such best-sellers as David Reisman's *The Lonely Crowd*, or novels like *The Man in the Gray Flannel Suit*, dreaded graduation, when we feared we would be recruited by a faceless corporation that would dress us in the standard suit and force us to conform to their mindless rules of speech and decorum while manufacturing superfluous products for the masses.

But the heirs of Jim Clyman, Jedediah Smith, and Kit Carson are hard to organize into a homogeneous mass, and Tocqueville underestimated the stubbornly anticonformist individualism imbedded in American character, even though he was the first to give it its proper name. He paid too much attention to that proper Bostonian, former President John Quincy Adams, who lamented that the wrong sort of person was populating the new States ("people for the most part without principles or morality, who have been driven out of the old States by misery or bad conduct or who know only the passion to get rich),"[35] while his own New England was populated by "enlightened and profoundly religious men." The people on the frontier are the real American heroes.

He also underestimated our creative talent. He would have had greater confidence in us, and avoided the embarrassment of announcing a dearth of literary talent in America, if only he'd read Whitman:

> Do I contradict myself?
> Very well then I contradict myself,
> (I am large, I contain multitudes.)

Americans are defined by the struggle between individualism and a dominant majority, and by many other tensions: we are "a society of laws, not men," but we adore flamboyant lawbreakers, from Jesse James and Dillinger to Bonnie and Clyde and the Godfather, from Thelma and Louise to Bill and Hillary Clinton. We echo Harrison Ford's words to Carrie Fisher in *Star Wars* when she calls him a scoundrel: "Scoundrel. I like that." We resent government intrusion, but we want government to do many things for us. We think it is wrong to meddle in other countries' affairs, but we want to support democracy and fight tyranny all over the world. Time and time again, Americans passionately hold conflicting ideals.

No wonder we're so busy all the time; we've got a lot of internal stress to work off. Notice that this national stress is precisely the opposite of the sort you hear about in the popular press, the kind of stress that comes from work. This is the sort of stress that *drives* you to work, because you must meet a very high standard, perhaps the highest standard ever demanded of a man. The Englishman Auberon Waugh put it in Tocquevillian terms:

> . . . equality is not some crude fairy tale about all men being equally tall or equally tricky; which we not only cannot believe but cannot believe in anybody believing. It is an absolute of morals by which all men have a value invariable and indestructible and a dignity as intangible as death.[36]

It's a spiritual stress, another of the fundamental tensions that define us. It has to do with religion, with Americans' relationship with God.

# CHAPTER 2

---

# RELIGIOUS FAITH ANCHORED BY SECULAR INSTITUTIONS

*There is no country in the world where the Christian religion retains a greater influence over the souls of men.*

To his great surprise, Tocqueville finds that the Americans, the most freedom-loving and materialistic people in the world, are also the most religious. Although he finds overwhelming evidence for this discovery, and although every serious contemporary investigation, survey, and public opinion poll confirm the fact, it remains one of his most surprising findings. It flies in the face of the conventional wisdom of the past two hundred years.

In the Old World, religion was part and parcel of the government. Not only did the traditional regimes base their rule on religious authority, but they brought the churchmen right into the heart of the state. Tocqueville's own France honored the great Cardinal Mazarin, one of the creators of the modern nation-state, and Henry VIII's England was in large part the intellectual masterpiece of Cardinal Wolsey (whose American descendant, James Woolsey, headed the Central Intelligence Agency in the 1990s, in one of those delightful occurrences with which the muse of history amuses herself). State ceremonies were held in the great cathedrals of Europe, kings and ministers paid obeisance to the leaders of their churches, and religious doctrine was codified in the laws and constitutions of their lands. Every country had an official religion and a state church.

The fortunes of religion thus quite naturally rose and fell with those of the national leaders, and when the great democratic revolutions of the eighteenth and nineteenth centuries attacked the old regimes, they attacked the churches at the same time. It was a short step from attacking the clergy to attacking their doctrines, and religion came to be considered a reactionary force. Revolutionaries and progressives were invariably anticlerical, and were often either deists or outright atheists.

Not so in America. To be sure, there are plenty of skeptics, deists, and atheists here; there's a bit of everything. But in America the spirit of liberty and the spirit of religion not only coexist, but nourish each other. The relationship could hardly be more complete or mutually beneficial, as Tocqueville proclaims: "Liberty regards religion as its companion in all its battles and its triumphs . . . it considers religion as the safeguard of morality, and morality as the best security of law and the surest pledge of the duration of freedom . . ."[1]

Tocqueville's words jar our ears, because, ever since the Enlightenment of the eighteenth century, most leading intellectuals have believed that religion and politics are logically and legally two separate realms, that the advance of liberty will eventually overwhelm religious beliefs, and that the two should be sharply divided. Our schools and newspapers and, from time to time, even our courtrooms are full of this misguided view of the proper relationship between politics and religion, but Tocqueville gives it the back of his hand:

> Religious zeal, said they, must necessarily fail the more generally liberty is established and knowledge diffused. Unfortunately, the facts by no means accord with their theory. There are certain populations in Europe whose unbelief is only equaled by their ignorance and debasement; while in America, one of the freest and most enlightened nations in the world, the people fulfill with fervor all the outward duties of religion . . . [2]

Indeed, Tocqueville tells us, the more democratic the political system, the more important is religious belief: ". . . . it is more needed in democratic republics than in any others. How is it possible that society should escape destruction if the moral tie is not strengthened in proportion as the political tie is relaxed? And what can be done with a people who are their own masters if they are not submissive to the Deity?"

Not to worry, Americans are spectacularly religious. By any measure—church attendance, membership in religious organizations, belief in God, belief in an afterlife—we are more religious than any other modern society. Some of the numbers are so remarkable that they seem divinely inspired, like the poll that found 94 percent of Americans believing in God (as compared with 70 percent of the English and 67 percent of the Germans).[3] Even the Ayatollah Khomeini would have been thrilled if his fellow Iranians demonstrated such an intensity of belief. Some 86 percent of Americans say they believe in the existence of heaven, exactly double the German percentage. Only a third of Tocqueville's fellow Frenchmen admit to belief in the devil, while more than double the number of Americans do, and nearly 80 percent of Americans consider religion "very or quite important" in their lives, compared to 45 percent of Europeans.

Modern social scientists are as astonished as Tocqueville at the religiosity of Americans. For them, American religiosity is rather like the old story about the bumblebee. All aeronautical engineers can show you with great precision that the bumblebee cannot possibly fly. But the bumblebee, blissfully unaware of the scientific evidence, flies anyway (and manages to collect a bit of honey while he's at it). Americans are the religious version of the bumblebee story. From Karl Marx and Max Weber to the latest college sociology texts, it is taken for granted—indeed, it has been proven in dozens of other countries—that as people become richer and better educated, they become less religious. We, blissfully unaware of this law of human nature, get richer and better educated, without losing our faith. Indeed, the richer we get, the more religious we become.

The sociologists and the political scientists have devised scales to measure both economic development and the intensity of religious belief, so that they can predict how a society will evolve. According to these forecasting tools, only a tiny fraction of Americans (5 percent) should give religion a major role in their lives.[4] Americans are a scientific impossibility: we have created the most advanced economy and remain the most religious people.

How can this have happened?

## A Uniquely Voluntary Religion

First of all, Christianity in America is quite different from the European varieties. We don't have major churches, we've got sects. We aren't so much Catholics, Lutherans, Calvinists, and Episcopalians as we're Baptists, Methodists, Quakers, and scores of lesser-known Christian evangelical denominations, not to mention the variations within the sects themselves (such as the regional differences among Baptists), or the messianic and utopian sects, from the Mormons to the Shakers, the Jehovah's Witnesses, and the Branch Davidians.

Here is another of those tensions that define American character: Just as we are driven by internal conflicts concerning the nature of freedom, so there are innumerable variations on the theme of Christian faith, each claiming divine authority. Who is right? This is no small matter, after all: the salvation of eternal souls is at stake. Americans don't settle such questions by theological debate (we'd immediately challenge the winner to a new debate); the answer has to come from results. We judge people's religion by the way they behave and, in keeping with our drive for success, by how well they do.

Once again, politics and religion embrace: the greatness of a society is a measure of the goodness of her religion, for God would not reward us if our worship were unworthy in His eyes. If, on the other hand, our society becomes more corrupt, if illegitimate births or drug use or pornography become rampant, it is a sure sign that we have strayed from the true path. Decadence is more than a shame; it is a warning that we are on the road to damnation.

Thus, from time to time we must undergo a spiritual purge and renewal. At the very moment Tocqueville sets foot in the New World there is an explosion of religious fervor, known as the Second Great Awakening. The country is swept by a veritable explosion of faith, spread by impassioned preachers claiming direct contact with the Almighty, and demanding that Americans rededicate themselves to the high moral calling of their religion. In keeping with the intimate relationship between religion and politics, the Great Awakening spills over into public life, producing a new moralism in politics (the Temperance Movement, campaigns against the dramatic increase in illegitimate births), a surge of concern for the poor and disadvantaged, and several utopian communities of the sort that the hippies of the 1960s knew well: a fusion of radical socialist social experimentation and a highly personalized religion. Finally, the Great Awakening strongly reinforces the moral revulsion against slavery, and becomes the language of the Abolitionists.

We replay this passion play with striking regularity,

invariably with explosive social and political consequences. The first Great Awakening, a century earlier,
shaped the generation of the Revolution and the Founding. The second, which Tocqueville witnesses, provided
much of the moralistic impetus for the generation of the
Civil War. The third Great Awakening, in the early years
of this century, provided inspiration for the great reforms
of the New Deal. Some believe that yet another national
religious revival was well under way by the early 1990s:
At the time of the conservative political landslide of
1994, such distinguished political thinkers as Walter
Dean Burnham and Robert W. Fogel suggested that the
Republican victory of that year was most likely due to a
fourth Great Awakening.[5]

An intimate embrace indeed. "Religion in America
takes no direct part in the government of society, but it
must be regarded as the first of their political institutions;
for if it does not impart a taste for freedom, it facilitates
the use of it."[6]

Our great religious variety permits Americans to seek
spiritual fulfillment in many different ways, a religious
variation on the theme of our celebrated individualism.
To be sure, the Pilgrim fathers were short on religious
toleration, and the founders of the original colonies certainly established dominant churches, but by the early
eighteenth century there were so many different sects—

even in New England—that it was impossible to speak of a single colonial theology. With so much competition among the denominations, preachers have to tailor their messages to their audience . . . or lose it. Tocqueville finds that religious leaders rarely challenge the opinions of their flock, except when the very existence of the church is at stake, and since public opinion is changeable, the sermons are, too.

Tocqueville rather likes this flexibility, but he knows that there's a dramatic downside to it. If religious leaders are simply going to cater to the whims of their congregants, if they are not going to chastise their followers for straying from the straight and narrow, then religion risks becoming just another version of social commentary. To avoid this humiliation, the churchmen, sooner or later, will have to insist on a hard core of divine truth. They will have to risk their popularity in order to assert the basic principles—moral as well as theological—of the faith.

This is especially true because American religion, like American politics, is voluntary. Nobody imposes religious participation on us any more than we are required to go to the polls and vote. It is a matter of custom and belief, not of formal obligation. Churches are one more example of that "collective individualism" Tocqueville discovered in our other civic activities. We generally join a larger religious community in our religious practice.

But not always; our individualistic approach to religion sometimes takes people of faith out of their churches in search of a highly personal religious experience. In recent years, for example, there has been a decline in church attendance, although not, at least according to the polling data, in religious belief or religious fulfillment. A deeply religious woman interviewed by the *Detroit News* in the summer of 1999 said, "I had a very bad experience with our church and left and never started going to another one. There are a lot more religion programs on cable and a lot more radio shows on the religious aspects."[7] Her church meets on cable. Call it a virtual church, another American invention.

Tocqueville's insight that American religion works hand in glove with other uniquely American expressions is marvelously illustrated by the St. John Coltrane African Orthodox Church in San Francisco, where the liturgy is based on the great jazz musician's spiritual music. "Congregants gather every Sunday for music-filled celebrations led by their own energetic saxophone-playing bishop, Franzo King." For those who might marvel at the adoption of a patron saint who was a heroin addict, Bishop King proclaims that Coltrane's "journey to cleanse himself physically and spiritually is a road that eventually took him to sainthood.[8]

Despite the great variety, and despite all the idiosyncracies of our religious practices, Tocqueville finds a near-universal consensus that religious belief is indispensable to the proper functioning of the country, and we often act as if any faith is better than no faith at all, a sentiment famously pronounced by President Dwight Eisenhower; "I don't care what a man believes, as long as he believes something." Jimmy Carter's U.N. Ambassador, Andrew Young, noted admiringly that the Ayatollah Khomeini, whatever his faults might be, was nonetheless "a religious man," and therefore worthy of some respect. The notion that some religious ideas might be dangerous, or even evil, is a rarity among Americans, and Tocqueville often remarks that American Protestants feel at home in almost any church, since the sermon rarely deals with doctrine, but concentrates on living a moral life and building the good society. Once again, politics and religion intersect.

Second, Edmund Burke was right when he called the Americans the "Protestants of Protestantism, the Dissenters of Dissent,"[9] for our driving passion for equality is at one with our religious convictions and institutions. The American sects are not formally structured as hierarchical organizations, but as congregational groups. Like our politics, our religion is based on consensus, and our religious institutions are remarkably "bottom up," rather than "top down." Moreover, American religion is quintessentially evangelical: most of us believe that God can speak to any man at any time. It is easier for us to think of ourselves as fundamentally equal when we see ourselves as equals in the eyes of God, and work together as equals within our churches.

Tocqueville thus recognizes that the idea of equality is far more than a political or legal matter; it is part of a religious vision that underlies the messianic nature of American politics and the democratic nature of American religion. Both are driven by the idea of equality and both encourage political democracy. Indeed, Tocqueville insists that American democracy cannot flourish without American religion, Like any other article of faith in a free society, religion stands on its own, and people either accept it or reject it on its own terms, not because it is imposed on them. The religions we accept are of a piece with our politics. "I do not know whether all Americans have a sincere faith in their religion—for who can search the human heart?" Tocqueville muses, "but I am certain that they hold it to be indispensable to the maintenance of republican institutions. This opinion is not peculiar to a class of citizens or to a party, but it belongs to the whole nation and to every rank of society."[10]

Third, American Christianity encourages our passion for material gain. The dark pessimism of European Calvinist predetermination brightened considerably in the

New World, and American followers saw their own material success as evidence that they were among the chosen few. The most popular sect, John Wesley's Methodism, was a vastly greater success in America than in England, and his message was a perfect fit for Americans' basic impulses: he urged his followers to get rich.

American religion reinforces enterprise, and success in this world is linked to a warm welcome in the next:

[Americans] sacrifice for a religious opinion their friends, their family, and their country; one can consider them devoted to the pursuit of intellectual goals which they came to purchase at so high a price. One sees them, however, seeking with almost equal eagerness material wealth and moral satisfaction; heaven in the world beyond, and well-being and liberty in this one.[11]

Nearly a century after Tocqueville, the great sociologist Max Weber reached the same conclusion: "The spirit of capitalism . . . was present before the capitalistic order." It was brought to America on the *Mayflower* by the Pilgrim fathers. In Weber's famous theory, our relentless drive to create wealth came from the terrible inner tensions created by the Calvinist doctrine of predestination: not knowing whether we are saved or damned, we desperately seek some sign that we are among the chosen, and material success is taken to be such a sign.

That is why our lust for wealth is unending; it is why even the most successful tycoons don't drop out and live the contemplative life on a Pacific island. They need constant reassurance that they haven't simply been kissed by Fortune; they need to know they have been blessed by God. We admire successful men, we truly believe they are among the chosen, and we want to share their grace. Years ago Walter Lippmann dryly observed that "we have always acted instinctively on the theory that golden thoughts flow in a continuous stream from the minds of millionaires,"[12] and a look at any best-seller list over the past half-century shows the staying power of this key element of our national character.

We believe that the winners get it all. Just as Tocqueville says, they've got wealth in this world and a first-class ticket to paradise. We emulate them because we believe they are chosen and we want to enter their ranks.

It sounds too good to be true, and it is. Christopher Lasch reminds us that "for those who take religion seriously, belief is a burden, not a self-righteous claim to some privileged moral status."[13] Like the vision that we can one day achieve full equality, our conviction that we can have earthly wealth and divine grace in a tidy bundle masks another internal turmoil. The Christian tradition is very suspicious of personal wealth. We often ignore all that talk about it being harder for the rich to enter heaven than for a camel to pass through the eye of a needle, or the poor inheriting the earth; but we know it is there. At a minimum our religious practice imposes rules on the ways in which money can be acceptably earned, as well as a strong insistence that wealth be shared with those less fortunate. Tocqueville knows that the wild pursuit of success can breed rampant selfishness, and that religion is necessary to remind Americans of their obligations to God and other men. We can't just race around getting rich by any and all means, and then proclaim that we're blessed; we need moral limits.

Like so much of American character, the internal push and pull between religious belief and material ambition is an unstable equilibrium, and we go over the edges from time to time. On the one hand, we sometimes chuck the rat race, opt out of the materialistic frenzy, and throw ourselves headlong into total religious experience. As Tocqueville predicts, we have a long tradition of utopian cults, often linked to exotic or downright mystical faiths. Some of us even follow maharishis to mountain communes and self-proclaimed prophets to the wilderness in South America, and others join the Shakers in chaste religious ecstasy. They invariably shrivel up and disappear, to be sure (the Shakers were down to eight survivors in late 1999), but new visions are always cropping up.

On the other hand, we are constantly in danger of having our religious passions overwhelmed by our lust for profit and luxury. One might think that abandoning religion would increase our frenzied quest for more, more, more, but Tocqueville insists the opposite: without the tension between faith and enterprise, we'd lose our dynamism.

> The reproach I address to the principle of equality is not that it leads men away in the pursuit of forbidden enjoyments, but that it absorbs them wholly in quest of those which are allowed. By these means a kind of virtuous materialism may ultimately be established in the world, which would not corrupt, but enervate, the soul and noiselessly unbend its springs of action.[14]

Unexpectedly, it turns out that our great energy is not simply the result of greed, as so many critics of American capitalism would have it, nor merely of a spiritual anxiety about our destiny in the world to come. A religious people that hails material success is—by definition—a bundle of contradictions. We can thank God for our contradictions; they make us great.

Tossing off this brilliant insight, Tocqueville drags us back to one of his basic themes: religion is more desperately needed in democratic countries than in more authoritarian ones. In nondemocratic societies, morality can be imposed by the rulers, but in a free democracy, where we make our own rules, we have to govern our own behavior. In one of his most lyrical observations, Tocqueville gives a ringing defense of the American melding of strong religious faith and secular freedom, turning it into a political axiom: "For my own part, I doubt whether man can ever support at the same time complete religious independence and entire political freedom. And I am inclined to think that if faith be wanting in him, he must be subject; and if he be free, he must believe."[15] Our strong faith provides the very foundation of our freedom, by inculcating the moral rules of an otherwise wildcat society. Faith gives us the certainties we need in order to launch ourselves on our course of creative destruction:

. . . In the moral world everything is classified, systematized, foreseen, and decided beforehand; in the political world everything is agitated, disputed, and uncertain. In the one is a passive though a voluntary obedience; in the other, an independence scornful of experience, and jealous of all authority. These two tendencies, apparently so discrepant, are far from conflicting; they advance together and support each other.[16]

Tocqueville, bless him, has a very rosy opinion of our moral behavior. He thinks we're the most ethical people on earth, he thinks that Americans are unusually monogamous and true to their spouses (which, breaking the American stereotype of the French, he finds wholly admirable), and he has a wildly optimistic view of American women. Religion sometimes fails to keep man's mischievous instincts in check, he says, "but its influence over the mind of woman is supreme, and women are the protectors of the morals."[17]

No doubt it was true in 1831, but things are different today. It's a good thing he doesn't go to the movies or watch TV. If he saw Madonna on the big screen, he might wonder about the supreme religious influence on the mind of woman.

He has been proven right about the religious underpinnings of American morality and American civic life. As usual, we put our money where our mouths are. We are the most philanthropic people on earth by a spectacular margin (in part because elsewhere, governments finance organizations, including churches, that are privately supported in the United States) and our generosity is doubly linked to religion: people of faith, in all income brackets, give a much higher percentage of their income to charitable causes (more than half of non-churchgoers give no money at all, while less than one-fifth of regular worshipers fail to give). Religious organizations are far and away the biggest recipients of our largesse (nearly half of all individual donations and more than four times the average contribution of the next largest category—health). These numbers are even more impressive when you recall that Ted Turner blew a billion dollars on the United Nations and Bill Gates added another billion for "minority" scholarships—hardly religious activities—and two billion dollars have a substantial effect on the distribution curve, even in America.

Tocqueville is also quite right to stress the vital importance of an orderly moral universe in a free and creative society. Without strict moral rules, we cannot fulfill ourselves as free people (one of those little paradoxes that are so often overlooked by those who misspeak in the name of an abstract notion of freedom). The most successful innovators in any endeavor invariably have a firm grounding in the rules they are about to transcend. Ask any jazz musician if he can improvise without a thorough mastery of the rules of his instrument and the rigid rules of chord and rhythm structures. Many of the greatest jazz trailblazers, from Goodman and Ellington to Brubeck and Monk and Marsalis, had classical training, and took pleasure in performing Mozart or Beethoven at the same time they were creating an entirely new set of rules. Or ask the creators of new algebras and geometries whether they could have imagined such things without first having mastered, and submitted to, Euclid's iron rules.

Creativity in political and intellectual life are similarly channeled into positive innovation by the firm boundaries of moral virtue. "Hitherto no one in the United States has dared to advance the maxim that everything is permissible for the interests of society," Tocqueville intones with approval. There are limits, fixed by the religious rules. And a good thing it is, too, because the "anything goes" doctrine, in Tocqueville's prescient words, "seems to have been invented in an age of freedom to shelter all future tyrants."[18]

That being so, we can no more take religion out of American public life than we can purge our souls of the profit motive. Indeed, as Michael Novak has argued (at one with Tocqueville), the two go together: "The more closely attuned to Christian and Jewish faith that its citizens become, the better democracy, capitalism and pluralism should function. As Tocqueville acutely noted, religion is the single most important political agency in democratic regimes . . ."[19]

But where does that leave those who argue that there must be an impenetrable wall between religion and civil society? And where does it leave American democracy if the religious foundations are weakened or cracked?

## CHURCH AND STATE

Tocqueville neither overlooks nor rejects the separation of church and state in American Constitutional law. He knows it well (he's a great fan of Jefferson), and greatly approves of it, as does virtually every religious leader he meets. It's just that he (along with Jefferson) doesn't believe for a minute that "separation" means the radical secularization of our public life.

The First Amendment forbids the creation of a national church and prohibits Congress from passing laws to restrict the freedom of religious practice. It does not require, or even foresee, the removal of official churches in the states (of which there were several, from Anglican to Methodist and Dutch Reformed, at the time of the Bill of Rights), let alone a series of laws designed to make society safe from religion. Several states barred Jews, Catholics, and atheists from public office more than half a century later, although the states eventually followed the federal example, The careful language of the First Amendment, and the practices of the time, were very far from our current reading, which banishes churches and indeed religious language from vast realms of public activity. It is hard for today's Americans to imagine that the "separation" doctrine was not designed to remove religion from public life, but to increase its freedom and importance. Just listen to two of our best historians on the subject: Michael Kamen, who reminds us that "church disestablishment . . . was not demanded by libertarian atheists but by evangelical pietists concerned with freedom of religion;"[20] and William McLoughlin, who flatly states that the practice was designed "to free America *for* religion, and not *from* religion."[21]

The separation of church and state was not codified by the American Civil Liberties Union, nor conceived by people who wanted their children protected from religion. Nothing of the sort was imagined. Education in America was seen, first and foremost, as moral education, and therefore entrusted overwhelmingly to men and women of the cloth. Until quite recently, religion was not only in the schools, it was central to the educational enterprise. As the country expanded West, the federal government required the new territories to provide for the religious education of the settlers. Tocqueville would consider quite mad anyone who suggested that there was the slightest constitutional basis for driving religion out of education, or any other public forum, and he would condemn the contemporary efforts to remove any trace of the Almighty from our history, such as this bit of nonsense from *Bon Appetit* magazine's special Thanksgiving edition, 1999: "As every schoolboy learns, the Pilgrims celebrated the first Thanksgiving to commemorate their successful harvest in the New World and to thank the neighboring Indians who had helped them survive a difficult first year." The schools may well misinform our children, but educated people know that the Pilgrims gave thanks to God.

To be sure, religious leaders stayed out of elective politics, either because they were explicitly forbidden to do so (by most states), or simply because, as Tocqueville notes, public opinion wouldn't tolerate it. He doesn't find priests or ministers in government because very few citizens would vote for them. We don't want our priests to govern, we want them to preach. Quite unexpectedly, Tocqueville finds this state of affairs enthusiastically endorsed by everyone he meets, above all by the religious leaders.

Over and over again, priests and ministers tell him that their popularity is significantly increased by their separation from politics. He is so impressed with their unanimous testimony that he underlines the paradox: religion in America has actually been strengthened by removing it from direct involvement in the affairs of government. "The real authority of religion was increased by a state of things which diminished its apparent force."[22]

Mind you, he's not talking about virtual religion. The Americans he knows and admires so much do not practice their faith by watching a TV evangelical; they shut down for the Sabbath and go to a real church. "On the seventh day of every week," Tocqueville happily writes, "the trading and working life of the nation seems suspended; all noises cease, a deep tranquility, say rather the solemn calm of meditation, succeeds the turmoil of the week, and the soul resumes possession and contemplation of itself."[23]

Once in church, the Americans are reminded of their moral obligations:

> He is told of the countless evils caused by pride and covetousness; he is reminded of the necessity of checking his desires, of the finer pleasures that belong to virtue alone . . . On his return home he does not turn to the ledgers of his business, but he opens the book of Holy Scripture . . .

A very different world from ours, and not just because few of us disdain the weekend sports spectacles and shopping malls in favor of Bible readings. It is different because religion permeates civic life, and is assumed to be in harmony with our individualistic democracy.

Tocqueville knows lots of people who want religion

driven right out of politics and society, but they are usually not Americans; they're the Europeans back in the Old World. Back there, if you are fighting for a freer society you are invariably anticlerical, and you're not likely to settle for a mere disestablishment of the national church. You want religion itself taken out of the marketplace of ideas, because your history and your personal experience have taught you that the priests are opposed to freedom. Even today, the battle between people of faith and radical secularists rages on all over Europe.

A hundred and fifty years after Tocqueville's quick trip to America, a series of court decisions and the effective political action of the advocates of radical secularism have taken us a long way toward institutionalizing the old European view of the relationship between religion and politics. At times, the ostentatious fear of religious influence on American life turns into a caricature of serious debate. Can we tolerate the display of the Ten Commandments in a courthouse? Can religious clubs use public school facilities for after-school meetings? Can communities have Christmas or Chanukah displays? Even less to the point, can anybody pronounce a religious thought in any public or quasi-public setting?

In Ohio, the ACLU filed a lawsuit . . . seeking an injunction to prevent coaches at London High School from encouraging their players to pray and listen to Bible readings at football meetings . . . The U.S. 5th Circuit Court of Appeals in New Orleans . . . ruled . . . that public school districts couldn't allow invocations (before football games . . . ).[24]

This dramatic change in public policy on religion has been accomplished in the past half-century. The systematic challenge to the Tocquevillian "intimate embrace" began very quietly right after the Second World War, in a 1947 Supreme Court Decision, *Everson* v. *Board of Education*, written by Justice Hugo Black. A New Jersey community had authorized the use of public funds to bus Catholic students to and from their parochial school, and a challenge made it to the Supreme Court. Two key phrases from his decision eventually broke the long honeymoon between religion and public service: "Neither a state nor the Federal Government can set up a church. Neither can pass laws which aid one religion, aid all religions, or prefer one religion over another." This was the opening wedge in a battle that rages throughout our institutions, from schools to courtrooms, from Congress to Hollywood.

Those who challenged New Jersey's practices probably got a lot more than they bargained for. They were upset at public money supporting students at Catholic schools, but the Court's language inevitably established a much broader precedent. Over the next fifty years, the opponents of religious discourse used it to expand their assault.

Tocqueville is not surprised at such warfare; he has lived through it in France, and foreseen it for us. He knows that advocates of unbridled freedom are always annoyed by religion, and he patiently counsels them to think again, because they have got it precisely backward. "When these men attack religious opinions," he warns, "they obey the dictates of their passions and not of their interests."[25] If they want true freedom, they must support a lively religious life.

With rare exceptions, the radical opponents of the intimate embrace between politics and religion did not gain much of a following in America until well into the twentieth century. (Mark Twain, who was one of them, never published his celebrated anti-religious essays during his lifetime, for example.) The public schools Tocqueville saw were all religious schools, firmly in Protestant hands. The first effective advocates of radical secularism in America came from the remarkable generation that survived the Great Depression, instituted the New Deal, won the Second World War, saved Western Europe, and responded to Soviet aggression by engaging in the Cold War. Their lives were quite different from those of their predecessors: instead of a peaceful and largely isolated existence in a prosperous America, they were subjected to a rapid series of terrible traumas, which had effects even more profound than those produced by the first great catastrophe of the twentieth century, World War I. The enormous misery of the depression raised the real possibility that the entire American enterprise was an empty shell. If this were not failure, what was? And if we had failed, where were we to look for new inspiration?

Inevitably, we looked back across the ocean, and we saw new and tempting experiments: Soviet communism, which attracted a large following among American intellectuals; Italian fascism, in which Franklin Delano Roosevelt himself found things to admire and perhaps imitate,[26] and even, for a short time, German national socialism, which was esteemed by the likes of Joseph Kennedy and others who fell for the illusion of racism.

All these European experiments—and the American tinkering that followed—shared a belief in a big, powerful and intrusive state, which would ensure that catastrophes like the Great Depression would not recur, and would exercise greater control over public policy to achieve a happier society. It fit nicely with necessity, because shortly after the depression we needed a powerful state, with a powerful army, to defend ourselves from those suddenly hostile European experiments that, one after another, threatened our existence.

It also fit nicely with the interests and ideas of a group that shared the "progressive" European suspicion of religion: American intellectuals, who had long envied their European counterparts and wished America were more like Europe. Intellectuals hold astonishingly high status in the Old World, while Americans have traditionally considered them marginal players in the great game. Intellectuals don't make nearly as much money as the real stars, they don't found new enterprises, they certainly don't command armies, and their products (books and essays) aren't as desirable as those of the "important" people. Predictably enough, the intellectuals tend to be hypercritical of America. Their alienation has little to do with economic misery, as Luigi Barzini found during a happy time, the Roaring Twenties:

> The more intelligent and articulate Americans, professors, writers, and journalists, or the well-read, well-traveled, and more discriminating, saw mainly the revolting vulgarity, the gross hedonism, the corruption rampant everywhere, and the stupid materialism. Many of them fled, as they had always done, abroad, to the Left Bank, or (the rich) to

sumptuous palazzi, *hotels particuliers*, and Medicean villas, where they could read the *Paris Herald*, and surround themselves with obsequious servants and fastidious friends.[27]

There is nothing new about this; most intellectuals see themselves as critics of their world, and treasure their independence of conventional thinking. And intellectuals are always tempted by the conceit that they, the most cultured people, are better suited to make the country's most important decisions than is the great mass of the electorate. It is considerably more attractive to be the *consigliere* of The Prince than to teach undergraduates or to write books and essays, even for the most prestigious publications. Once American intellectuals started to gain the ear of the political elite, they were able to advance their pet projects, including a more intrusive and centralized national state and, as one of the powers of the newly expanded state, the removal of religious discourse from as many public fora as possible.

Daniel Patrick Moynihan has pointed out[28] that the Supreme Court Justices who most vigorously (mis)used the First Amendment to authorize the assault on religious expression—Douglas and Black—were very strongly anti-Catholic. Justice Douglas relied on a book on Catholicism that simply stated:

Our American Freedoms are being threatened today by two totalitarian systems, communism and Roman Catholicism. And of the two in our country Romanism is growing faster than is communism and is the more dangerous since it covers its real nature with a cloak of religion.[29]

To be sure, the anti-religious actions have been carried out by a minority. As Tocqueville found, and as public opinion polls and the spontaneous action of the American people consistently demonstrate, the overwhelming majority of Americans do not agree with the anti-religious intellectuals and judges and would not want them to govern the country, any more than they want religious leaders to govern. The war over American religion has not remained one-sided; outside the citadels of the intelligentsia, there is something approaching a popular revolt. The Moral Majority, which had so much political clout in the 1980s, was in large part a response to Jimmy Carter's instructions to his Justice Department in 1978 to take a hard look at the tax exemptions of religious schools. A charter school movement in Michigan in the late 1990s attracted national attention and enthusiastic parental support because of its outspoken endorsement of religious-based moral values. Many rodeo competitions begin with a prayer. Texas authorities challenged a 1999 court decision banning prayer in the team locker room or on the sidelines before the game begins. And, as a writer from Midlothian, Virginia, noted:

> Few (religious) excursions can match the bluegrass festival, where God, man and the Mason Jar mingle most gracefully. These congregations of bluegrass musicians and enthusiasts . . . also teach a largely overlooked lesson: Low-church Protestants, lately infamous for putting Darwin in a Kansas doghouse, really do know how to let their hair down.[30]

This is not just nostalgia at work; one of the bands at the bluegrass festival reported that their gospel albums sold three times as well as the secular ones, and religious books routinely outsell those on our fashionable bestseller lists.

Some of our political leaders are resisting the effort to drive a wedge between religion and public life. Both Vice President Al Gore and Texas Governor George W. Bush have called for "partnership" between government and religion (thereby overlooking the wisdom of Ronald Reagan's dictum that the eleven scariest words in the

English language are "Hi! I'm from the government and I'm here to help you").

Tocqueville recognizes that liberty and democracy are threatened whenever the influence of religion is weakened. If we were to become fundamentally different, if we lost our religious underpinnings, then our moral compass would break, we would be lost, and the American mission would fail. As Barzini puts it, the greatness of America rests on Biblical virtues: "resolution, loyalty, courage, sobriety, a sense of duty, tenacity, prudence, moderation, thrift, love of one's neighbor, and fortitude."

> Could the fading of the Book as an inspiration for all seasons, could universal wealth and the abolition of risks, fatally weaken, one day, the moral fiber of the Nation? . . . If the moral fiber weakened, what could take its place? Avarice, the hunger for power, psychoanalysis, transcendental meditation?[31]

Tocqueville worries about the decline of religion, but, given his understanding of the depth and vitality of American religion, it is not one of his principal concerns. As for the efforts of the radical secularists to emarginate religion, he fears a strong, politically active church far more than one that has been driven out of public places.

> I am so much alive to the almost inevitable dangers which beset religious belief whenever the clergy take part in public affairs, and I am so convinced that Christianity must be maintained at any cost in the bosom of modern democracies, that I had rather shut up the priesthood within the sanctuary than allow them to step beyond it.[32]

Tocqueville knows that we can survive and even flourish with a corrupt elite. Corrupt elites are a commonplace, as is mediocre leadership, and we've outlasted them all. The greatest threat to our freedom comes from the corruption of the people themselves. Tocqueville's great fear is that, driven by our frenetic quest for material gain, we will lose our religious convictions, thereby sabotaging the moral restraints that both stimulate us and channel our explosive energies in positive directions. That would be the equivalent of punching a hole in the pistons of our national engine, or, as he puts it, uncoiling the springs that energize us. We must constantly be reminded, he nags, that "it is only by resisting a thousand petty selfish passions of the hour that the general and unquenchable passion for happiness can be satisfied."[33] So long as we are strong in our faith and resist temptation, we will remain exceptional.

But he still hasn't told us how we manage it.

# CHAPTER 3

---

# RUGGED INDIVIDUALISTS WITH A GENIUS FOR COOPERATION

*If men are to remain civilized or to become civilized, the art of association must develop and improve among them at the same speed as equality of conditions spreads.*

We do it through that seeming oxymoron, collective individualism. We organize ourselves to deal with our problems, instead of waiting for others, or our own political and social institutions, to solve them for us.

And a good thing it is, too, because a highly individualistic society is a tyrant's dream. As Tocqueville ruefully reminds us, a dictator exerts all his efforts to separate us from one another, so that he can more easily dominate and oppress us. Dividing us makes it easier to conquer us and force us to submit to his will. Stalin, the master tyrant of our time, set the Soviet people to spy on each other, thereby shattering any semblance of social cohesion, and rendering the Soviet peoples unable to resist his terror.

Our proud individualism puts us at risk of losing our freedom. It is all well and good to make the Lone Ranger a national hero, but it took an army to win our independence from Great Britain, and to defend it against Germany, Italy, Japan, and the Soviet Union. No matter how tough and brave, a bunch of individuals couldn't have managed it, nor can they manage it when overly ambitious American leaders challenge our freedom. We need collective enterprises not only in those emergencies that present us with the stark option of hanging alone or surviving together, but as a matter of course. We need a sense of collective mission in our corporate life as in our foreign policy, in our politics as in our families.

Without common efforts, we are too weak to defend ourselves against would-be oppressors or outright enemies, whether from within or without. Singly, we may achieve short-lived personal glory, but we are ultimately impotent unless we band together. "The vices which despotism produces are precisely those which equality fosters," Tocqueville intones, and thus another of those inner tensions: "despotism is more particularly to be feared in democratic ages."[1]

He's reminding us, in different words, that since we instinctively prefer equality (the mother of individualism) to liberty, we'd better guard against the dangerous consequences of this tendency.

The dangers of individualism are not only political, for a society based on equality leaves people to fend for themselves. Pursuing our separate personal fortunes in our frenetic way, we have a tendency to isolate ourselves from one another, and to draw into our shells. We do it even when the working day draws to a close. Tocqueville observes with bemused surprise that Americans prefer to go home and get drunk in private to going to public places to drink with their friends and neighbors. This is individualism with a vengeance! More seriously, frenetic individualism not only weakens our ability to advance the common good, but stunts our own growth, because our ability to fulfill our human potential depends upon working together. Tocqueville launches into an uncharacteristically emotional analysis: "Feelings and opinions are recruited, the heart is enlarged, and the human mind is developed only by the reciprocal influence of men upon one another . . . these influences are almost null in democratic societies . . . and this can only be accomplished by associations."[2]

Not that he thinks we're facing a present danger; indeed, he's convinced that we've found the perfect solution. "The Americans have combated by free institutions the tendency of equality to keep men asunder, and they

have subdued it."[3] In a dialectical way, we have resolved the tension between individualism and our messianic common mission by a uniquely American
practice: working together on the myriad little problems
that afflict us.

Somebody gets an idea, and pretty soon there's an
organization to advance it. Tocqueville was amazed to
find a hundred thousand men swearing to go on the
wagon. At first he thought it was ridiculous; why didn't
they just sit quietly at home and drink water by themselves, if that was the way they felt? But then he realized
that they were concerned about a wave of alcoholism,
and they had decided to do something about it. We are
still trying to do something about it, and about similar
addictions as well, through organizations like Alcoholics
Anonymous. Nor does it stop there. We have thousands
of rehab centers, special "farms" where addicts can be
kept from all temptation, church groups to provide positive reinforcement, hot lines, crisis centers, and door-to-
door volunteers to guard against backsliding.

Sometimes these private organizations become very
large indeed, from giant corporations like Microsoft to
vast not-for-profit associations like the American Association of Retired Persons. Some become public companies, others remain private; some last for centuries,

others, their mission either failed or completed, disband themselves.

Never mind a hundred thousand men giving up devil alcohol; roughly half the adult population of the United States engages in volunteer work. Only 18 percent of Americans admit to belonging to no voluntary group or private association, while more than 60 percent of Tocqueville's countrymen are nonjoiners. And we are not losing our taste for association; quite the contrary. Of the million or so charitable or nonprofit associations providing social services in the United States in the mid-1990s, more than two-thirds were created within the past thirty years. As always, there is a strong religious component. Drucker calls many of these organizations "para-churches," because they are religiously inspired or otherwise linked to religious organizations.

Some of our associations are very serious, while others verge on slapstick. When we worry about the quality of education, we form organizations like the PTA. We have Mothers Against Drunk Driving. On the other hand, we also have the likes of the National Organization Taunting Safety and Fairness Everywhere (NOTSAFE), which launched a campaign to ban milk when it was found that prison inmates drank more of it than normal citizens did. When we get excited about our baseball or football teams, or movie stars, or even our first names, we form fan clubs and frolicsome organizations with mock-serious names, like Mikes of America or Bobs International.

One such organization has become a macabre self-fulfilling prophecy: BLOOP, the Benevolent and Loyal Order of Pessimists, which puts out a short reading list (Orwell, Camus, Sartre) and issues Certificates of Pessimism to sufficiently gloomy citizens. Their annual meeting takes place on Income Tax/Titanic Sinking Day, an appropriately gloomy date that has attracted a dark cloud overhead. One year an honoree was struck down by lightning and, as the *Economist* pointed out with macabre satisfaction, two journalists working on BLOOP stories died "in tragic circumstances" shortly afterward.[4]

But, for the most part, our organizations are designed to solve real problems. Whether getting out the vote or cleaning up downtown, stopping gang violence or recycling newspapers, we, the vaunted individualists of the United States, roll up our sleeves and join in.

How did we get this way? Tocqueville is baffled. Most of our habits came from England, but the English don't form associations. Their society is based on traditional divisions, and they behave quite differently from us: "The English often perform great things singly, whereas the Americans form associations for the smallest undertakings."[5]

If it didn't come across the Atlantic on the *Mayflower*, perhaps our remarkable penchant for creating associations stems from a deeper cause. After all, people have made common cause from the origins of human history, leading Aristotle to conclude that man is a "political animal." Serious contemporary thinkers like Frank Fukuyama and Lionel Tiger have provided anthropological, historical, biological, and sociological evidence for this theory, but Tocqueville is not convinced that this explains us. How to account for the people (and they are in the majority) who don't spontaneously organize themselves? He certainly doesn't think that Americans are just like everyone else (only Americans in an age of political correctness believe such silliness), since he can plainly see that most other countries (including his own) don't do any such thing. There does seem to be a global tendency to form associations outside the traditional sphere of government, but it is a recent trend, and, insofar as others are moving in this direction, they are copying us, not the other way around. If the formation of associations were simply an expression of the common genetic code of *homo sapiens*, it would have been a constant in human history. But it isn't. It started here.

It's an American invention, and the tones of admiration, verging on awe, in which Tocqueville talks about the way we create associations show he considers it extraordinary: he hails it as a rare triumph of emotion and intellect. Rare indeed; it's the central nervous system of the entire American enterprise. "In democratic countries the science of association is the mother of science; the progress of all the rest depends upon the progress it has made."[6] For once, Tocqueville chooses his words poorly; it's art, not science.

We have carried this art to a new level, undreamt-of even by the most avid Aristotelian, and we've done it despite our strong individualistic inclinations to remain apart from one another. We do it in our typically paradoxical fashion: by breaking down the traditional boundaries between men. We scrap old-fashioned manners and go straight to the point. Americans "attach more importance to intentions than to forms,"[7] he says, and we do indeed. "He meant well," excuses a multitude of social offenses. We are too busy to master the old rules of etiquette, and we are far more inclined to overlook boorish behavior than are members of more traditional societies. Even today, failure to address a member of the European, Latin American, or Asian upper classes in precisely the proper way can end all hope of friendship, or even a good working relationship.

We don't worry about such trifles, but we do worry about feelings. When an American meets another person, he immediately tries to find out what sort of person the other is. "Where is he coming from?" is the first order of business. Having abandoned the manners that keep a certain distance between people, we constantly probe one another, trying to find an emotional or intellectual basis for cooperation. Associating with one another isn't just a way of advancing a cause; it's the way we bond. Drawing together for a specific purpose, we want to work with people with whom we can share both our ideas and our civic passions, thereby developing our minds and enlarging our hearts. All our causes, large and small, whether the crusades of three world wars in this century or saving abandoned house pets in our neighborhoods, are emotionally charged. Aristocrats in past times shouldered their civic burdens out of a traditional sense of duty: *noblesse oblige*. We do it to hasten the creation of a perfect world.

From the PTA to IBM, from NOTSAFE and BLOOP to the American Civil Liberties Union and the American Association of Retired Persons, our associations are driven by the same passions and tensions that led the Donners and the Reeds to organize their wagon train to California, and that have led us to dominate the world. We have gained a lot, and hope to gain it all, but the downside is heartrending:

In democratic times enjoyments are more intense than in the ages of aristocracy, and the number of those who partake in them is vastly larger; but, on the other hand, it must be admitted that man's hopes and desires are oftener blasted, the soul is more stricken and perturbed, and care itself more keen.[8]

It should therefore not surprise anyone that we elect our leaders as much for the emotions they inspire as for the policies they advocate. When Bill Clinton tells us that he feels our pain, we resonate, because it's painful to be an American; we have a lot invested in our success, and we suffer our failures and constant frustrations. When Christopher Lasch decries the contemporary trend toward a "therapeutic society," and excoriates us for sinking into self-indulgence, he's got the concept right, but the timing is all wrong. It's not something that came in with the baby boomers, or their parents, it's not the result of Freudianism or even Doctor Spock. We've always been intensely involved in our personal success and salvation, and we've always been in therapy of one sort or another.

On the other hand, the upside is glorious. When it works right, America produces a fuller emotional life than past societies, and enriches traditional institutions in surprising new ways.

## FAMILIES AND FRIENDS; MEN AND WOMEN

Read the letters between children and parents in non-democratic societies, Tocqueville urges, and you will find a formality of address that reproduces the deference shown to the upper classes by their inferiors. As are all other relationships in societies based on inequality, family ties are based on traditional notions of superiority and inferiority: men superior to women, parents superior to children, older child superior to younger sibling. These are not merely customs or mores; they are written into law.

In America, family bonds are based on emotion (and, Tocqueville adds, respect for age). There is no formal way of addressing one another. Between husbands and wives, and parents and children, there are scores of nicknames, and affectionately sarcastic titles. Above all, there is an easy candor ("the language addressed by a son to his father is always marked by mingled freedom, familiarity, and affection . . ."), and respect is earned, not merely ceremonial, just as it is in the broader society: ". . . the conventional, and the legal part of parental authority vanishes and a species of equality prevails around the domestic hearth."[9]

Just as we recognize each other's freedom in society

at large, so our children are granted their freedom at an appropriate age, and without great struggle. "The father foresees the limits of his authority long beforehand, and when the time arrives, he surrenders it without a struggle." And this willingness to grant responsibility to our children enables us to achieve a rare intimacy. Tocqueville's admiration palpably slides into envy: ". . . the relation of father and son becomes more intimate and more affectionate; rules and authority are less talked of, confidence and tenderness are often increased, and it would seem that the natural bond is drawn closer in proportion as the social bond is loosened."

Tocqueville finds relations among American siblings similarly excellent, both because of the ease and candor of American life, and above all, because there is no law of primogeniture: the wealth of the father is divided among the sons, not given *en toto* to the eldest. This removes the most divisive force in traditional family life. The sons know that each will have his fair share. Under these circumstances, the brothers are bound together by common interests and genuine affection: "it divides their inheritance, but allows their hearts and minds to unite."[10] Then another epiphany: "The remarks I have made on filial love and fraternal affection are applicable to all the passions that emanate spontaneously from human nature itself."

All our associations are emotionally charged. The American family is the smallest example of the art of association, and it embodies the mutual respect, the willingness to compromise, and the emotional bonding that characterize our most successful organizations. Those of us fortunate enough to have, or to have been raised in, such families can testify to the strength, tranquility and, as Tocqueville says, the sweet intimacy they can provide. But these families are becoming scarcer, to our regret and our peril.

In fact, they were much rarer than Tocqueville thought. Even in Puritan New England, two generations before Tocqueville arrived, some 30 percent of all births were premarital.

But "premarital" means that they invariably got married, because otherwise father, mother, and child would have suffered an enormous social stigma. Nowadays that stigma has vanished, and we no longer hear about "shotgun marriages" in which the impregnating male is compelled to save the honor of the woman he got pregnant. Moreover, that the very word "family" is regularly conjoined with other words like "single parent" and "same sex," Tocqueville would find preposterous, since he knows that the strength of the family, and the character of future generations, rests upon the contributions from both father and mother. As the great historian William

McNeill puts it, the subversion of the family, and the drastic erosion of nurture by a full family, means that "institutions of all kinds—public and private, governmental, religious and social—have been undermined."[11]

The big change, of course, has to do with women, and therefore with men.

It will have been noticed that Tocqueville talks about fathers and sons, not mothers and daughters. They are not discussed in the chapter on family life, but get separate treatment, just as they did in early nineteenth-century America. Tocqueville offhandedly remarks that women do not hold public office, and do not run businesses. They take care of the house, and provide the moral pillar without which no society can long survive. A sexist patriarchy, in short.

And yet Tocqueville believes that our singular prosperity and strength is due, above all, to the superiority of our women.[12] Moral superiority above all, of course, for "morals are the work of women," and, as he well knows (although he omits it), that "work of women" greatly involves the rearing of boys, so that they grow to be moral men. He finds American women better educated, intellectually more interesting, and morally more virtuous (or so he is convinced) than their European counterparts, and he loves it. He is particularly enthusiastic about the fact that American women are not sheltered from the seamy side of life. Since the society is so open, it is impossible to wall off the women from the facts of life. They consequently learn all about it at an early age, and enter marriage with a fairly realistic view of the nature of men and of the rough world with which they're going to have to cope. Indeed, the prenuptial American woman has many of the same characteristics of her husband-to-be. Somehow, she voluntarily sublimates her ambitions and funnels them into her roles as wife and mother.

Tocqueville marvels at the strength and character of the American woman, and never so much as when he encounters her on the perennial testing ground of American character: the frontier. There he finds well-educated and well-to-do women living in the most daunting circumstances, and yet their inner fortitude shines through.

Fever, solitude, and a tedious life had not broken the springs of their courage. Their features were impaired and faded, but their looks were firm; they appeared to be at once sad and resolute. I do not doubt that these young American women had amassed, in the education of their early years, that inward strength which they displayed. . . . The early culture of the girl may still therefore, be traced . . .

under the aspect of marriage; her part is changed, her habits are different, but her character is the same.[13]

This almost superhuman person clearly would not eternally tolerate a subordinate role in American society, and, although he dreads it, Tocqueville sees that the liberation of women is just around the corner. He thinks it will be a disaster: "by . . . attempting to make one sex equal to the other, both are degraded, and from so preposterous a medley of the works of nature nothing could ever result but weak men and disorderly women."[14]

Wrong! We certainly got weak men, but the new women were anything but disorderly. They were ambitious, disciplined, and overachieving. Indeed, women are now predominant in American society (to take the clearest indicator, solid majorities of college and graduate students are female, which guarantees the women will dominate the next generation), to the point where thoughtful scholars are wondering how to save the men. In a classic case of unexpected consequences, men have been liberated from a whole set of moral obligations, starting with those attendant to fatherhood. Nowadays, if a woman tells her boyfriend that she's pregnant, he can simply say, "How nice for you," and walk away. While there may be a financial cost to this total inversion of roles, he will not be faced with the choice of being cast out of society or heading the new family. She will head it, alone.

However we sort out the consequences of empowering women, it will require our art of association, for it is as fascinating, perplexing, and potentially ruinous a challenge as we have ever faced. Typically, it is a task we have created for ourselves, which is the usual reason for our associations: we draw together because the challenges we set ourselves are too great to be accomplished by a single person, and we prefer to do it ourselves rather than have the government do it for us. Tocqueville shudders at the thought of asking government to do even more than it does already, even for the noblest cause.

Over and over again, Tocqueville warns of the terrible dangers of bigger government: not only restrictions on our freedoms, but the corruption of our souls. We can abandon ourselves to a government that will gladly make these agonizing decisions for us, in exchange for our liberty, or parts of it. We are constantly offered that Faustian bargain. It is not hard for Tocqueville to see it coming: when no man is able to be self-sufficient, and others have to produce the necessities of life, the government automatically seeks to bring the new processes under control. As government never voluntarily restricts its appetites, we have to organize to protect ourselves against expanding governmental power.

Associations snatch power from the jaws of government, and keep it in our hands. But the struggle for power is unending, a constant and stern test of our national character.

> The more [government] stands in the place of associations, the more will individuals, losing the notion of combining together, require its assistance: these are causes and effects that unceasingly create each other . . . The morals and the intelligence of a democratic people would be as much endangered as its business and manufactures if the government ever wholly usurped the place of private companies.[15]

Tocqueville didn't need Max Weber to know that the ethic of democratic capitalism was present in America long before the industrial revolution brought capitalist institutions to this continent. Nor did he need to witness the catastrophes of twentieth-century communism and fascism to know what happens to free societies when their governments seize control of economic and social initiative.

We are certainly not immune from the creation of a meddlesome government; our governors have always loved to tinker with us. Tocqueville remarks with astonishment and alarm that authorities in Massachusetts are trying to limit the use of tobacco, and he finds scores of examples of government-created companies to conduct and regulate commerce on our rivers and Great Lakes, and to build highways and other public works. He grants that many of these projects are worthy, and finds some of them even glorious. But he worries that government appetites are growing, and cautions us to resist bigger government with all our energies. He knows that we are intuitively opposed to bigger government, but he also knows that we, like all other great peoples, can be corrupted.

Tocqueville also understands, with laser-like precision, that the great American creation of the art of free association is revolutionary, and is fundamental to the success of any modern democratic society. As Peter Drucker so elegantly reminds us, with the exception of America, modern history has been the story of the "subjugation of all competing centers of power by one central authority."[16] We stood alone against this tidal wave, and before Tocqueville's eyes, we created new centers of power and new organizations, culminating in the giant business enterprises whose powers now dwarf many formerly mighty countries.

We didn't need to live through the "information revolution" to know that multiple centers of creativity are better than central planning; our multiple centers of creativity developed its component parts and set in motion the entire revolutionary mechanism. Just as we battered the old, centralized regimes into reluctant change, so we have unleashed our creative destruction on the world once again.

Even on ourselves. Tocqueville lived through the French Revolution. He saw innocent people jailed and guillotined in the name of democracy's creative destruction. He warns that unbridled freedom plummets wildly toward chaos and anarchy, the struggle of all against all in a revolution gone mad. We are not immune to this lethal infection of our souls; thus far, we have avoided it because of good leadership, good character, and good fortune. We did not need a bloody revolution to establish a free society, because America was made by a free people whose religious faith and driving ambition made it possible to work out the habits of a responsible democracy on a virgin continent. There, we had additional advantages of time and space: time to work out the details without invaders seeking to dominate us, and space in which to indulge in innumerable failed social and political experiments without involving the entire society. We knew that communism didn't work more than a century before Lenin, because we had tried it at Brook Farm and other egalitarian utopias.

But luck can turn, and the destructive impulses are strong within us. Robert Bork and Gertrude Himmelfarb[17] fear we are perilously close to freefall, having, in Himmelfarb's elegant play on words, de-moralized America. Both Bork and Himmelfarb are at one with Tocqueville in cringing at the spectacle of associations that promote the worst forms of self-indulgence, from the pornography and violence of music and cinema to the self-centered behavior of professional athletes, and the licentious and lascivious transgressions of President Bill Clinton.

When Tocqueville asks himself how to restore faith in a society that has lost it, he gives an answer that he knows will not find favor in the political class; the only hope is for the leaders of the society to behave as if they were believers. Virtue is much more than its own reward, Tocqueville preaches, for without a sound moral code, resting on religious faith, American character will be subverted and American democracy will fail.

If Tocqueville was distressed by Andrew Jackson, imagine his reaction to Bill Clinton.

It follows that it is folly to permit any and all associations to exist. Freedom of association may be one of the bedrock principles of American democracy, but even the freest society needs limits.

... unrestrained liberty of association for political purposes is the last degree of liberty which a people is fit for. If it does not throw them into anarchy, it perpetually brings them ... to the verge of it. .... I doubt whether, in any country or in any age, it is wise to set no limits to freedom of association.[18]

Tocqueville does not spell out the rightful limits on association, but we know him well enough by now to be able to deduce what they are. He dreads organizations that threaten the moral basis of society, and those that attack freedom itself. He loathes slavery in all its forms, and would shut down any association seeking to restore it.

He does not think such limitations of free association are dangerous to freedom, because such forbidden associations work for the ultimate destruction of freedom itself.

Above all other free associations, Tocqueville prizes the press. Where the people are sovereign, ideas must freely circulate, even when many of those ideas are dangerous and even though the press sometimes disseminates lies. Without a free press, our associations could not exist, because they would lack the information and opinions that drive us to band together.

Tocqueville is not a blind lover of the press; he recognizes that the media are biased, unreliable, and even scurrilous. Contrary to the beliefs of many contemporary press critics, the media have not fundamentally changed over the past century and a half. He gives us a portrait of the American journalist that could be written today:

> The characteristics of the American journalist consist in an open and coarse appeal to the passions of his readers; he abandons principles to assail the characters of individuals, to track them into private life and disclose all their weaknesses and vices.[19]

Gary Hart or Richard Nixon couldn't have put it more strongly or more accurately. Tocqueville's advocacy of freedom of the press is a choice of the lesser of two evils. For all its faults, the press (itself an association) provides us with the information around which we create our associations, and without the associations American freedom is doomed. The saving graces of the American press are that it is varied, decentralized, and independent of government control. Whatever the intentions of the media chieftains, we can get different views, and lots of information. To those who want to limit the freedom of the press in order to avoid at least some of its noxious effects, Tocqueville replies that this particular baby can't

TOCQUEVILLE ON AMERICAN CHARACTER

be cut in half to satisfy two mothers. You either get it all, warts and beauty marks included, or it won't survive. ". . . There is no medium between servitude and license; in order to enjoy the inestimable benefits that the liberty of the press ensures, it is necessary to submit to the inevitable evils that it creates."[20]

But we don't have to love it, and we must remain alert to its dangerous abuses. Above all, Tocqueville dreads a centralized press, because it could come to wield more power than any other American institution. In the 1960s and 1970s, this seemed a real possibility, as the major television networks and most of the leading newspapers presented a remarkably homogeneous view of the world. With striking consistency, leading journalists, editors, and producers have voted overwhelmingly for the Democratic Party's presidential candidate since the late 1960s. Nearly 90 percent of them voted for Clinton in 1996. The media acquired enormous power, sufficient to destroy two presidents (Johnson and Nixon), and had clearly become an integral part of the governmental establishment. Like the Executive, Legislative and Judiciary branches, the media fought for its own policy positions, supported its favored candidates and slandered those it disliked, and sought to destroy those who fought back. As a symbol of their full membership in government, journalists opened offices within government agencies, even in Langley, Virginia, in the buildings of the once-secret Central Intelligence Agency. They had arrived, and Tocqueville's worst fears seemed to have been realized.

Yet, by the mid-1980s, the networks were in a steep decline, the major newspapers were steadily losing subscribers, and an impressive number of new sources (first, talk radio, then internet sites) had emerged, with quite different political and social attitudes. As the numbers of the new media grew, the power of the old centralized networks decreased, to the great benefit of the citizenry. Contrary to what we might have feared a generation ago, the press today is very much the way Tocqueville describes it.

But this leaves unanswered the obvious question: If some associations should not be permitted, who decides which ones to shut down? This question cannot be answered by an appeal to "rights" or "freedoms," for rights and freedoms are precisely what are at stake. We are back to the basic tension that associations were supposed to solve in the first place: we can do it ourselves through democratic politics, or we can ask the government to do it for us. We know we should do it, but this requires that we devote time and energy in the public arena, and it causes pain, because the issues involved are complicated and stressful.

That is why we are still tempted by the Faustian deal. The government can make things simpler, and ease our tensions. It would be contrary to our character, but others have succumbed.

Happily, we have an antidote.

## SELF-INTEREST, RIGHTLY UNDERSTOOD

We find fulfillment, albeit strained and never fully satisfying, in our work, our religion, our families, and our associations, as well as in solo acts of heroism and creation. Simultaneously individualists and good citizens, creative destroyers and good family members, we have a public philosophy that explains and inspires our willingness to temporarily sacrifice our personal pleasures in order to advance a common cause. Tocqueville has a pompous name for it: "self-interest rightly understood." Big words for a simple thought. We don't appeal to lofty ideals to get our fellow citizens to join our associations. We appeal to their self-interest, tempered by common sense. We don't invoke profound philosophical principles when we ask others to help the poor; we say "we will all be better off by improving their lot." In Tocqueville's words,

The American moralists do not profess that men ought to sacrifice themselves for their fellow creatures because it is noble to make such sacrifices, but they boldly aver that such sacrifices are as necessary to him who imposes them upon himself as to him for whose sake they are made.[21]

We call it "doing well by doing good." By improving others, we improve ourselves.

Tocqueville quotes Montaigne: "Were I not to follow the straight road for its straightness, I should follow it for having found by experience that in the end it is commonly the happiest and most useful track." It's an enlightened civic pragmatism, an understated public philosophy for a democratic era that requires public service from all of us. If we realize that we advance our own interests by advancing the common good, we are therefore willing to give up time and money to assist others in improving their lot. We do it in the normal course of events. Although it's quite extraordinary, we don't brag about it. "In the United States hardly anybody talks of the beauty of virtue, but they maintain that virtue is useful and prove it every day."

Careful! Although Tocqueville is full of admiration for our virtuous pragmatism, he rather suspects that we're not quite as down-to-earth and commonsensical as we like to appear. He knows us well. It's quite true that we love to explain our actions in terms of self-interest, but we're a messianic people given to vast dreams and global missions. Disinterested and spontaneous impulses of virtue and generosity are natural to men everywhere, Tocqueville reminds us, and we have not suppressed these passions. It's just that "Americans seldom admit that they yield to emotions of this kind; they are more anxious to do honor to their philosophy than to themselves."[22]

This clever masquerade cloaks the basic tension between our passion for personal fulfillment and our mission to create heaven on earth. We are simultaneously driven in both directions, which is why we insist on limited government and maximum individual freedom but also demand vigorous action from the government to assist us in our efforts. It is the usual, amazing balancing act, a high-wire tour de force.

Tocqueville insists that we do not suffer from split personality, although it often seems that way. "At one time he seems animated by the most selfish cupidity, at another, by the most lively patriotism. The human heart cannot be thus divided." We have embraced both passions, in the way Tocqueville so well understands: we *freely* embrace our civic obligations, we insist on freedom in order to pursue our self-interest, which we advance by forming associations that advance the common good.

The Americans believe their freedom to be the best instrument and surest safeguard of their welfare; they are attached to the one by the other. They by no means think that they are not called upon to take a part in public affairs; they believe, on the contrary, that their chief business is to secure for themselves a government which will allow them to acquire the things they covet and which will not debar them from the peaceful enjoyment of those possessions which they have already acquired."[23]

Above all, we love big challenges, as befits a messianic people. Late last century the great historian Frederick Jackson Turner announced the closing of the frontier; there was no more free land in the United States. He suspected that we were at a major turning-point, because henceforth our explosive energies would be contained in a closed system, and would most likely create damaging internal tensions. In time, thrown inward upon ourselves, we might lose the frontier spirit that had driven us from one ocean to the other and had been the bedrock of our entrepreneurial genius. But the turn of the century did not mark a limitation of American character.

It was, on the contrary, the beginning of the American century. We lifted our vision and sought new frontiers, both physical and intellectual. Jim Clyman's spirit went to the moon with Neil Armstrong.

We're back to the Americans and the bumblebees. The bumblebee can't fly, but does, and we keep doing things that are theoretically impossible. Time and again it has been perfectly obvious to our critics and our enemies that we just couldn't overcome another obstacle, only to find that we've done it.

- Remember the vogue of Japanese-style capitalism in the eighties, which, according to a bevy of fashionable intellectuals, was destined to buy America and leave us in its dust? We took them for a ride, whether in the celebrated Pebble Beach Golf Course caper (sold to the Japanese for a billion dollars, repurchased a few years later at half the price) or the automotive industry, which responded to better and cheaper Japanese cars by producing even better and cheaper American ones. Today, the Japanese are struggling to achieve minimal economic growth, and all the top foreign automobile companies manufacture here;

- Remember the oil sheikhs of the seventies who, according to the usual suspects, were going to buy America with their petrodollars? Today they're scrambling to pay their bills, while we lend them our own abundant dollars;
- Remember the fanciful European expectations of dominating the world market with the "Euro"? They quickly learned that competition with America is a lot harder than simply creating a single currency.

It's dangerous, even fatal, to underestimate us. The Nazis called us a mongrel nation, suitable only for domination by a superior race. The Japanese warlords thought they could knock us out with one mighty sucker punch at Pearl Harbor. The Soviet Communists thought we were the avatars of a doomed system, destined to finish on the dustheap of history. One of their leaders, Nikita Khrushchev, proclaimed that he and his comrades would bury us.

The graveyards of decades recently past are full of arrogant tyrants who underestimated our strength and resolve. They were not destroyed by a single, exceptional generation; their doom was delivered over a span of four American generations. They misjudged American character, and went to ruin. They did not understand the amazing power of collective individualists facing a serious challenge.

We were lucky, too.

# CHAPTER 4

---

## ISOLATIONISTS CALLED TO INTERNATIONAL LEADERSHIP

*An aristocratic nation that in a contest with a democratic people does not succeed in ruining the latter at the outset of the war always runs a great risk of being conquered by it.*

Napoleon preferred a lucky general to a brilliant one, and the same sound principle applies to peoples as well. By that standard, it's only right that we've arrived at the top, because we've been blessed with good luck ever since Columbus discovered an unexpected land mass en route to the Indies. Maybe we're being rewarded for our religiosity; H. L. Mencken once remarked, with appropriate awe, that God protects the blind, the drunk, and the United States of America.

Even so, we've had more than our fair share of good fortune.

Our good luck begins with our fortunate location: our

two big oceans make invasion by would-be conquerors almost impossible, which is why we have nearly always felt invulnerable to direct attack. Moreover, our land is not only remote from danger, but good for planting, harvesting, digging, and drilling: we've got rich farm land and fabulous natural resources, from precious minerals to big, strong rivers and abundant forests. Tocqueville thinks that this enormous natural abundance, lying in wait for anyone who has the wit and the will to take it, is the primeval basis for American democracy. "Not only is legislation democratic, but Nature herself favors the cause of the people."[1] He, too, looks upon America as a Divine gift, offered to us at the precise moment when mankind had learned how to exploit natural riches, and needed space to create "an asylum for repose and freedom. Just then North America was discovered, as if it had been kept in reserve by the Deity and had just risen from beneath the waters of the Deluge."

Our luck continues with our neighbors, who have neither the desire nor the means to threaten our survival. Our first neighbors, the Indians, were easily driven out of their native habitats, beaten by vastly superior might and organization, and then reduced to misery. Our subsequent and present neighbors, the Canadians and the Mexicans, threaten us only with cheap labor and low-cost goods, not with armed aggression. No wonder we have great difficulty understanding most other countries, who are bounded by hostile neighbors with large appetites.

Imagine if we had the Red Army across the border to the north, and a big Syria, armed to the teeth, on the far side of the Rio Grande! We wouldn't have the luxury to indulge in our many political and social experiments; we'd be worried about making it to the next year in good shape. As it is, we're so laid back that we're blissfully unconcerned about the emerging military might of the People's Republic of China, even though the Chinese regime makes it quite clear that it intends to challenge us once it has become powerful enough.

Even apparent bad luck has usually worked to our advantage: the weather, for instance. Tocqueville may think that we live in some kind of earthly paradise, but there is a distinct downside to our location: We have uniquely violent weather, from tornadoes and hurricanes to blizzards, droughts, and searing heat. "Three quarters of the world's twisters touch down on our soil . . . There is a higher concentration of lightning strikes along the Front Range of the Rockies than anyplace else on the planet."[2] It has always been that way; evidence of ancient natural catastrophes abounds in the soil, in tree rings, ice cores, and even in Indian villages, long since obliterated by forces more terrible than anything brought by the white man.

Neither settlers nor slaves were prepared for the harshness of the American climate, as proven by the need for new English words to communicate the violent weather. It killed a lot of settlers, and was so devastating to the West African slaves that the slave owners moved south, to more temperate regions. The bad weather in the North and in the backwoods kept America at least half-free of slavery, a bit of good fortune that enabled us, two centuries later, to have a critical mass of people willing to fight against the slave states.

Bad weather toughened the New Englanders, and later the pioneers, who overcame incredible climatic hardships as they moved West. And bad weather got Americans thinking about the relationship between climate and human civilization. We've long suspected it was our fault:

Both Cotton Mather and Thomas Jefferson were convinced that the colonists had changed North America's climate by clearing off the virgin forests: global warming theories circa 1690 and 1770. Notions that the weather is behaving bizarrely because of something we have done to it crop up again and again in our weather history.

If the time allocated by evening television news broadcasts is an accurate indicator, the weather occupies much more of our attention than foreign policy does. That is a luxury reserved only for very lucky peoples.

Our enemies are far away, our neighbors are downright friendly, and we're doing very well. Why worry about the rest of the world?

Yet we do worry, albeit in our usual conflicted way. We have a love-hate relationship with the outside world. We hate it and fear it, because we all came from some foreign country where we were treated badly, and we came to America believing that we would find something better for ourselves and our children. We succeeded, often beyond our wildest expectations, and so we all know, deep within our national genome, that things are better here, and there is danger of contamination back where we came from. With rare exceptions, the only happy American expatriates are intellectuals who resent American success; the great movement of people is into America, not out of it.

This century has driven home that instinctive dread, because we have been dragged into three world wars and two "peacekeeping missions" in Europe, at an enormous cost in money and blood. And although we have saved the Europeans from their own suicidal inclinations, we have been contaminated by them, above all in the growth of a centralized state that Tocqueville dreads and that the Founders hoped they had prevented.

We also love the Old World, and not only in our secret yearning for royalty and aristocracy that occasionally bursts into blind infatuation with families like the Kennedys, or the importation, stone by stone, of London Bridge to the banks of a river in Texas, or the creation of the pseudo-aristocratic shooting clubs we met back in the first chapter. Barzini, who was raised in a society replete with aristocrats and royal families, of course sniffed it out: "the compulsive and impatient rush toward the West, the ever-retreating perfect future, always went with an aching and disproportionate yearning for the East, the past they did not have or had rejected."[3] It's hard being a revolutionary country; fatigue and even despair sometimes set in, and we look back over our shoulders and wonder if it's worth it.

To our built-in ambivalence, we add an ideological conflict. We know we have created the best political system, and we want to see the rest of the world adopt it. We instinctively root for anyone who challenges tyranny, and we put pressure on our leaders to support the challengers. And we do it in a highly idealistic way, forgetting how difficult it is to move from tyranny to democracy. Tocqueville, who lived under various forms of government, does not forget, and enviously mutters

"The great advantage of the Americans is that they have arrived at a state of democracy without having to endure a democratic revolution, and that they are born equal instead of becoming so."[4]

But we also believe that it is wrong to meddle in the internal affairs of other countries, and this conviction combines with our dread of foreign contamination to make it very difficult for the United States to use its power overseas until and unless some dramatic event occurs.

These two conflicting passions help explain why, when we do get involved, we generally convince ourselves that we are engaged in a righteous crusade. The conviction that we are doing the Lord's work helps us paper over the explosive tension, which has invariably exploded in our political debates over foreign intervention. We never think in the old, European terms of simply advancing our national interest: we wage holy wars, or we don't fight at all. Whenever we have leaders who fancy themselves masters of statecraft, and try to conduct a purely pragmatic foreign policy, they come to ruin. The American people will not long tolerate it, as Richard Nixon and Henry Kissinger found to their dismay. No matter how brilliant the stratagems, Americans need to believe that they are "engaged in a crusade to improve not their life alone but the whole world."[5]

Whatever we do, we invariably wait until the very last minute, paralyzed by the tug-of-war that exists within every American. We do not feel obliged, as do normal countries, to constantly prepare for the next war. We have *never* been ready for the next war. As far back as 1846, when we were on the verge of launching a two-front war to expand into Texas, California, and Oregon, the Congress was planning to close the Military Academy at West Point, thereby establishing a pattern that still shapes our decisions. Whenever a war is over, we dismantle our military establishment, because we are the first people in human history to believe, in the teeth of all the historical evidence, that peace is the normal condition of mankind. No doubt this foolish and perilous bit of naive wish-fulfillment comes in part from our radical egalitarianism: we like to think that all people are basically the same. Since we don't want war, we assume that others feel the same way. They don't. Even Tocqueville doesn't. "I do not wish to speak ill of war," he thoughtfully informs us in his most aristocratic tones, as "war almost always enlarges the mind of a people and raises their character." It's actually good for us, "in some cases it is the only check to the excessive growth of certain propensities that naturally spring out of the equality of conditions."[6] Tocqueville may think that war is a useful therapy, but our antidemocratic enemies don't see it that way. The Japanese didn't bomb Pearl Harbor to improve our character. They wanted to destroy us.

As the great strategic thinkers have invariably observed, war is terrible indeed, but peace has dangers of its own. Machiavelli thought it almost impossible for great political leaders to emerge in peacetime, and our own experience has born it out. Our greatest presidents were wartime leaders: Washington, Jackson, Lincoln, Teddy Roosevelt, Wilson, FDR, and Reagan.

When the survival of the country or the success of a glorious cause is at stake, all other concerns become secondary, and even those with the most talent abandon their preferred vocations and throw themselves headlong into the struggle. That is why our first generation was so remarkable, as Tocqueville recognizes. During the Revolution, and immediately afterward, the challenges were so enormous and the potential gains so great, that our spirits "were roused to the height which their great objects required." We remember Tocqueville's dictum that, in peacetime, our best minds and spirits pursue wealth in business, not glory on the battlefield or in electoral campaigns. We must now add an unexpected caveat: Big challenges bring out the best people, as the Revolution did. "In this general excitement distinguished men were ready to anticipate the call of the community, and the people clung to them for support and placed them at their head. But such events are rare . . ."[7]

When we're threatened, everybody rallies to support the country, as if they were involved in a great national association. No news here; everybody does it. Otherwise lackluster armies notoriously fight with great passion to defend the motherland. But ours is not the kind of nationalism that exists elsewhere. In other countries national identity revolves around a common ethnic origin, or a shared religion, or some preposterous notion of race. We are not nationalistic in that way; it's just not possible for a society as wildly diverse as ours. If there is any model for the way in which we feel part of a larger unity, it is the ancient Roman Republic, because our shared identity is a common citizenship, not a common ancestry.

But Romans were more class-bound than we are, their freedoms were more restricted than ours, and the allegiance of the citizens was an obligation, not a free decision. Our patriotism is inspired, not compelled. Only a mean-spirited intellectual could say that American patriotism is the last refuge of the scoundrel; Tocqueville recognizes it as the natural and admirable consequence of a free society of equals.

How does it happen that in the United States, where the inhabitants have only recently immigrated . . .

where they met one another for the first time with no previous acquaintance; where, in short, the instinctive love of country can scarcely exist; how does it happen that everyone takes as zealous an interest in the affairs of . . . the whole state as if they were his own? It is because . . . [t]he citizen looks upon the fortune of the public as his own, and he labors for the good of the state, not merely from a sense of pride or duty, but from what I venture to term cupidity.[8]

Our unique patriotism underlies the remarkable energy we show when challenged; since we feel ourselves integral parts of a common enterprise, we are willing to make sacrifices, even extraordinary and ultimate sacrifices, to ensure the enterprise's survival.

Tocqueville takes this principle one step further, and adds another of our peculiar inner conflicts. First of all, he notes that Americans hate war. True, our history of armed expansion to the West shows that we are a people of conquerors, but that was an unavoidable means to the usual end of creating more wealth. We do fight, but only when we're convinced it's necessary.

It generally takes an enemy attack to convince us.

We were dragged into the First World War when German U-boats torpedoed passenger ships on the North

Atlantic. We were providentially bombed into in the Second World War by the Japanese at Pearl Harbor, just in the nick of time. (Congress, in a typically wrongheaded mood, had tried to abolish military conscription the previous summer, only failing by a single vote.) Stalin underestimated our resolve at the end of the World War II when he meddled in Turkey, Greece, and Iran, thereby provoking the Cold War. The Russians, Chinese, and North Koreans concluded we would not fight for South Korea, and the North Korean invasion dragged us into the Korean War. Saddam Hussein was sure we would not fight him if he annexed Kuwait and menaced Saudi Arabia, thereby provoking the Gulf War.

Barring such exceptional circumstances, we like war even less than politics, and "the choicer minds of the nation are gradually drawn away from the military profession, to seek by other paths distinction, power, and especially wealth."[9] The quality of our military inevitably erodes in peacetime, as the armed forces become just another bureaucracy, and seniority, rather than talent, becomes the basis for advancement. Our military leaders are not only less talented, but older, and therefore "after a long peace . . . the army is always inferior to the country itself."

On the other hand, we love military leaders:

No kind of greatness is more pleasing to the imagination of a democratic people than military greatness, a greatness of vivid and sudden luster,
obtained without toil, by nothing but the risk of
life.[10]

That seemingly snide "obtained without toil," deserves
our attention. Tocqueville precedes it by observing that
we "are much less afraid of death than of difficulty,"
since difficulty thwarts our drive for wealth and personal
satisfaction, and makes us perennially frustrated. We are
back to Jim Clyman and the Donners once again. The
mountain men and the settlers who followed them were
quite willing to risk their lives for the glories of the West,
but they were often poorly prepared for the real obstacles
en route. So it is in warfare. We are reluctant to do the
hard, tedious and dirty work to get ready for war, but
once it is forced upon us, we fight ferociously, even bril-
liantly.

When a war has . . . roused the whole community
from their peaceful occupations and ruined their minor undertakings, the same passions that made them
attach so much importance to the maintenance of
peace will be turned to arms . . . Hence it is that the

147

selfsame democratic nations that are so reluctant to engage in hostilities sometimes perform prodigious achievements when once they have taken the field.[11]

Moreover, the outbreak of war shatters the bureaucratic regulations and enables talented people to rise rapidly through the ranks, quickly producing a new, younger team of leaders. "The principle of equality opens the door of ambition to all, and death provides chances for ambition." We may not be ready for war, but we catch up in a hurry.

Those who fight us had better be prepared to deliver a knockout blow right away, as was demonstrated by the Somali warlords who managed to kill a few Marines and drag the cadavers through the streets of Mogadiscio in front of the world's television cameras. If they give us time—and our leaders have the resolve to see it through—it will go badly for them. Throughout this century we have been extraordinarily lucky: our enemies did not understand our character. At every major turning-point, we have been attacked early enough, and with insufficiently lethal effect, to permit us to mobilize in time to win.

Tocqueville would never make the mistakes that cost the Kaiser, Hitler, Mussolini, Tojo, Stalin, and Saddam so dearly, because he knows that the fully-mobilized energies of a free people are superior to those of authoritarian regimes. If we're not beaten early, we're heavy favorites to win . . . unless, as in Vietnam, the war drags on for a very long time, and, contrary to our legend, we fail to win. In that case our insistence on quick results may overwhelm our craving for victory. As Tocqueville puts it, "The people are more apt to feel than to reason; and if their present sufferings are great, it is to be feared that the still greater suffering attendant upon defeat will be forgotten."[12]

To make matters worse, we're very slow to recognize danger. We're like the people in the sleepy towns in Jimmy Stewart's Western movies. In *Fire Creek* Stewart plays a bland, maddeningly reasonable and anticharismatic sheriff who fails to respond when a bunch of murderous thugs, led by Henry Fonda, intimidate the town. Stewart fights back only after they have killed an innocent young fool, appropriated the best-looking young girl, and threatened to take over the whole town. Stewart fights bravely, and with last-second help from a courageous woman (of the sort Tocqueville so greatly admires), carries the day.

It's heartwarming, but it's no way to conduct foreign policy in the real world.

Tocqueville knows a thing or two about war and bloodshed. An ancestor stood with William the Conqueror at Hastings, and his maternal father and grand-father were sent to the guillotine during the French Revolution. He knows with the certainty of death that every country has enemies, and that survival often requires habits of mind that are contrary to American character.

[A] democracy can only with great difficulty regulate the details of an important undertaking, persevere in a fixed design, and work out its execution in spite of serious obstacles. It cannot combine its measures with secrecy or await their consequences with patience. These are qualities which more especially belong to an individual or an aristocracy; and they are precisely the qualities by which a nation, like an individual, attains a dominant position.[13]

It's very hard for us to define a long-term strategy, and harder still to conduct it with patience and perseverance. We're an impatient people, after all, even in our national sport. Corporate executives are under constant pressure to produce results, and quickly, even if it might make more sense for the company to sacrifice short-term gains for far greater middle or long-term profit. We want to see large black numbers on the bottom line. So it is in foreign affairs; we expect our leaders to deliver positive results. If we invest men and money in a particular policy objective, we want a good return. Never mind that it is often prudent to spend money for weapons that are never used, or that governments are supposed to protect us against worst-case scenarios that never happen, instead of having to react to crises when and if they arise. We are a dynamic people, and we want action.

Knowing our weaknesses, Tocqueville can see that we will conduct foreign policy in fits and spasms, not with the patient cunning recommended by the grand masters of the art. We are more inclined to "a sudden effort of remarkable vigor, than for the prolonged endurance of the great storms that beset the political existence of nations."[14] Our best leaders try to prepare us for the exigencies of international affairs, while our worst give in to our weaknesses, and make no pretense of serious strategic planning. Thus Warren Christopher, the first secretary of state in the Clinton years, summoned the top officials of the Department of State, and told them not to expect any strategic vision from the Clinton Administration. "We do not have one," he briskly informed the diplomats, "and we do not want one. We will simply deal with problems as they arise." He, his successor, and his president, were true to these words.

This fundamental component of American character is

often blamed on the emergence of the electronic mass media. How can we expect our leaders to remain calm— even if inaction is clearly the best policy—when the news networks are showing us awful pictures of dreadful events? Television may be a cool medium, but it generates heated responses, and a clamor for action.

It's a tempting argument, because Americans love to blame failures on some vast, irresistible change—a technological innovation, in this case—but it's just a cheap excuse for mediocre leadership. When Tocqueville says we're more inclined to feel than to reason, he's not talking about the effect of the evening news. He's talking about the way we are. There are always calls for action, always demands for short-term fixes, always condemnations of leaders who seem to dawdle or blither.

It's sometimes better to dawdle, but you'll have a hard time convincing the American people, once they've gotten emotionally involved in some exciting foreign development. That means that good leaders will sometimes have to fight against the powerful force of public opinion. If they're simply going to read the poll numbers and enact policies accordingly, who needs the executive branch?

Tocqueville knows that it's hard to conduct a rational foreign policy in America, but he also knows from first-hand experience that it can be done, even in the teeth of public outcry. He reminds us about George Washington's behavior during the French Revolution, when there was a firestorm of public opinion demanding that we side with the revolutionary government and rally to the French against England. This was just a few years after our own revolution against His Majesty's government, and we were wildly enthusiastic about the overthrow of the French monarchy. Moreover, France—in the admirably charismatic if questionably democratic figure of the Marquis de Lafayette—had supported us in the Revolutionary War, and we wanted to repay the favor. Washington, however, believed that it was none of our business, and wanted to stay out. He was accused of harboring secret monarchist sentiments (indeed the popular press of the day even suggested that he planned to become a sort of American king himself). But he remained calm, resisted the public clamor, and eventually earned the undying admiration of his countrymen because he kept us out of a potentially ruinous war.

Tocqueville happily describes Washington's resistance to public opinion as a triumph of prudence over impulse, and the implementation of a mature design rather than "the gratification of a momentary passion."[15] Washington's farewell address to the nation, in which he warned against involvement in foreign conflicts, became an enduring keystone of American policy, which Tocqueville calls "eminently expectant; it consists more in abstaining than in acting." We hear it resonate in many voices, from those opposed to Manifest Destiny and our adventures in Mexico and the Philippines, to those fearing contamination from our allies and neighbors in NAFTA in the 1980s and 1990s.

Tocqueville's words describe one side of our conflicting impulses: stay out of other countries' affairs. The opposite impulse is equally strong, and just as imperative: do everything possible to spread democracy and bring down tyranny. Both have been part of our character since the founding, but the second impulse required the emergence of America as a global power before it came into play. Tocqueville's admiration for George Washington's prudence is certainly appropriate for a small, relatively weak and fledgling democracy, tempted to intervene against the mightiest military power in the world. It would have been madness for the United States to get involved in the global conflict of the late eighteenth century, no matter how strongly we were drawn to support revolutionary France.

Even the most ideological country must make some accommodation to the brutal calculus of power, and Tocqueville is right to admire a tough-minded president who knew how to repress our revolutionary instincts so that we could focus on the first stage of our historic mission. We had to build America first, then accomplish the triumph of democracy over the enemies of equality.

But that was then. With his astonishing gift of prophecy, Tocqueville knows things are going to change dramatically, in large part because of our amazing good luck. We are going to get much bigger, as we fill out the continent and gobble up the Hawaiian Islands and buy Alaska from the Russians. We are also going to get stronger, as our entrepreneurial energy and our industrial savvy generate the wealth necessary for the production of military might. There is no one to stop us except ourselves. To be sure, Tocqueville is no naif; he does not expect that we will arrive at our historic rendezvous without having to suffer. We will undoubtedly have to overcome some major obstacles, even domestic convulsions (Tocqueville is very clear-eyed about the explosive consequences of slavery), but he is confident we will emerge from them with our character intact: "Nor will bad laws, revolutions and anarchy be able to obliterate that love of prosperity and spirit of enterprise which seem to be the distinctive characteristics of their race . . ."[16]

Once all that has been accomplished, the other half of our character—the part of us that impulsively and passionately leaps to the defense of freedom wherever it is at risk—will come into play. No longer impeded by our youthful weakness, we can continue our national mission beyond the boundaries of our national frontier. If Tocqueville is right when he prophesies that the idea of equality will destroy the old order, we, the carriers of that idea, will have to be its foot soldiers.

## THE GLOBAL DEMOCRATIC REVOLUTION

The relentless growth of a democratic country could never have succeeded in the Old World. First and foremost, are the enormous differences in national character. There is no European equivalent of Jim Clyman. There were some in England—Lawrence of Arabia is the prototype, and Margaret Thatcher a more recent model—but the English did not have our miraculous geography. The British Isles were too small for them to fully express their genius, and their frontiers were perforce overseas, in India and Africa and the Middle East.

If there were an American-style democratic republic in Tocqueville's Europe, it would never have been given the time to become rich and powerful. No sooner had the French Revolution toppled the Bourbons than the monarchical armies of the continent marched toward

Paris. We were saved from ruin by our geographical fortune, and have been given that rarest of all blessings: the luxury of making errors without paying a terrible price for our follies. Our blunders are embarrassments; those of democracies with hostile neighbors are likely to be fatal.

For the first time in human history, a singularly diverse people has been given the chance to experiment with a new kind of society, inhabited by a new kind of man, driven by a new kind of ethos. Tocqueville guesses that we will have about a century to flex our muscles on the North American continent and prepare for our destiny. It would be churlish for us to quibble over the details; his crystal ball is luminously clear. We were torpedoed into World War I about eighty-five years after he sat down to write *Democracy in America.*

He also foresaw our nemeses: our archetypal opposites, the very incarnation of tyranny. The Russians.

The American struggles against the obstacles that nature opposes to him; the adversaries of the Russian are men . . . The Anglo-American relies upon personal interest to accomplish his ends and gives free scope to the unguided strength and common sense of the people; the Russian centers all the authority of society in a single arm. The principal instrument of the former is freedom; of the latter, servitude . . . each of them seems marked out by the will of Heaven to sway the destinies of half the globe.[17]

Tocqueville not only calls it right, he's fully understood the stakes. More than a century before the event, Tocqueville knew that the conflict between Russia and America, like the Second World War before it, was far more than a traditional battle for territory or strategic position. The Soviet Union was not just an enemy country, it was the antithesis of freedom or, as Ronald Reagan accurately put it (paraphrasing Tocqueville): the evil empire. The Cold War was an epic ideological struggle between two messianic superpowers, each convinced that God (or, for the Russians, the course of history) was on its side. Had the Soviet Union won the Cold War, servitude would have spread around the world. Our victory gave freedom a rare opportunity.[18]

It goes without saying that Tocqueville also understands that modern conflicts are far less likely among democratic countries than between nations governed by diametrically opposed systems. He fully agrees with those who insist that the spread of democracy is a major benefit to our national security. Indeed, his main hope for Europe is that some variation of the American model will spread in a single stroke to all the major countries, thereby making possible an extended period of peace.

And so it was. Europe was granted peace in 1945 by the greatest democratic force in history: the American Army that imposed democracy on the defeated tyrannies of the continent after the Second World War. At first it was an uneasy peace, menaced by the Soviet Empire across the Yalta Line. Nearly half a century later, with the defeat of the Soviets, the threat of another great European war passed into history.

## CONTAMINATION

Tocqueville had feared that we might not be equal to our historic challenge, that in the big showdown, the Russians would win and freedom would fall to servitude. He knew our weaknesses, above all our urge for a quick fix instead of a steady, patient strategy to fulfill our national mission. This translates into lack of long-term vision; each event, every challenge, is treated as a separate problem rather than part of a larger pattern. "Perseverance is maintained only by a distinct view of what one is fighting for . . . But it is this clear perception of the future, founded upon judgment and experience, that is frequently wanting in democracies."[19]

Tocqueville's fears were well founded, for the Cold War was not like the previous two world wars; we could not win it with a single, intense effort. It required real resolve, and a constant reminder of what we were fighting for. Remarkably, we kept our eye on the long-term goal for half a century, and found a great leader who managed the complicated end game with firm resolve.

We found it more difficult to deal with victory.

One might have expected a great national celebration when the Soviet Empire crashed, but our leaders acted more embarrassed than triumphant. President Bush and Secretary of State Baker repeatedly urged the satellite states of the Empire to remain subservient, and whenever Gorbachev's power was challenged—as in the memorable failed coup of 1990—top American officials instantly called their Russian counterparts to shore up the failing regime. At every step of the dismemberment of the Soviet Empire, American leaders, enthusiastically egged on by most leading intellectuals and the stars of the popular press, cautioned against the dangers of triumphalism in the West. Hardly a voice was heard to ask: "but should we not rejoice in our triumph?" After all, we *had* won a splendid victory, freed hundreds of millions of people from oppression, and created unprecedented opportunities for the advance of democracy.

No doubt most Americans saw it this way, as did those who had worked with Reagan to make it happen, but there was an enormous effort by a significant part of the political and intellectual elites to pretend that we had *not* won. Some credited Gorbachev with having brought down his own system, while others saw the fall of Communism as a purely internal process.

And what about the last big Communist regime, the only country in the world that could conceivably threaten our survival in the new century? In the 1992 election campaign, Bill Clinton was highly critical of the Bush administration's softness toward the People's Republic of China, and promised a more vigorous approach if he became president. But within a few months of entering office, Clinton proved far worse than his predecessors: he not only dropped any criticism of the Chinese regime, but actively armed China. Clinton embodied all the dangerous weaknesses against which Tocqueville warns us: the lack of long-term vision, the search for quick, attractive fixes to complex long-term problems, the blithe pretense that there is no need to prepare for future conflicts.

Although arming China was something quite unprecedented (never before had an American leader taken extraordinary steps to arm a potentially lethal enemy), many of Clinton's failures were a sad repetition of our past. Only a great leader could have kept us focused on foreign policy after the Cold War; lacking an obvious threat, we happily turned our energies to the completion of the American experiment. Tocqueville would not have been surprised, for he had foreseen the pattern.

But that was not his only fear. While he worried that we would eventually fall to an enemy better prepared and more determined than ourselves, he dreaded the effect war would have on us. He realized that war, even a victorious one, would threaten our freedom, and thereby menace our national enterprise. He had it just right:

> No protracted war can fail to endanger the freedom of a democratic country ... War ... must invariably and immeasurably increase the powers of civil government; it must almost compulsorily concentrate the direction of all men and the management of all things in the hands of the administration. If it does not lead to despotism by sudden violence, it prepares men for it more gently by their habits. All those who seek to destroy the liberties of a democratic nation ought to know that war is the surest and the shortest means to accomplish it.[20]

Short of domination by our enemies, there are two ways that war can destroy our freedom: either by a sudden act of violence (such as the proclamation of a state of emergency that justifies granting emergency tyrannical powers to the government), or by a more gradual process that prepares us for tyranny "more gently," by changing our habits to accommodate the demands of an ever more intrusive and demanding government. This process is well under way, just as Tocqueville foresaw.

With every major war, the federal government grew more powerful and more intrusive, limiting our businesses, directing our education, monitoring our movements and our communications, even driving religion out of major sectors of our public life. This is precisely the process we have long feared from foreign involvements, the sort that makes us more like the people from whom we fled in the first place and against whom we have fought throughout the twentieth century.

Tocqueville dreads it, because he knows it can ruin everything.

# CHAPTER 5

─────◆─────

# APOSTLES OF FREEDOM
# TEMPTED BY LUXURIOUS
# TYRANNY

*It is indeed difficult to conceive how men who have entirely given up the habit of self-government should succeed in making a proper choice of those by whom they are to be governed . . .*

Tocqueville is full of admiration for our good works, our great energy, and our messianic vision, but he is under no illusion that our character contains only positive forces. With a ruthless accuracy worthy of the biblical prophets, he sees that we are quite capable of doing ourselves in, and wrecking the whole American enterprise. Just as the greatness of America is due to the unique character of its people, the ruin of America is built into our minds and souls.

Tocqueville has repeatedly warned us against a potentially fatal weakness in our character: we're so hell-bent

164

on the extraordinary benefits we gain from equality that we pay insufficient attention to liberty. Engrossed as we are in the pursuit of our personal fortunes, we lose sight of the necessity of devoting our energies to politics, both in public office and through our private associations. A free democracy is not immune to the threat of tyranny; indeed, quite the opposite is true: "I am not so much alarmed at the excessive liberty which reigns in [America] as at the inadequate securities which one finds there against tyranny."[1]

Tocqueville anticipates one of the most profound analyses of American destiny, the Lyceum speech of Abraham Lincoln delivered in 1838, a scant five years after the publication of *Democracy in America*. Lincoln asked rhetorically what could bring down America? An invading army from across the oceans? Not at all:

All the armies of Europe, Asia and Africa combined . . . with a Buonaparte for a commander, could not by force, take a drink from the Ohio, or make a track on the Blue Ridge, in a trial of a thousand years.

At what point then is the approach of danger to be expected? I answer, if it ever reach us, it must spring up amongst us . . . If destruction be our lot, we must ourselves be its author and finisher. As a nation of freemen, we must live through all time, or die by suicide.

As always, we are torn in two directions at once. Our commitment to equality pulls us toward a majoritarian conformism that threatens to suffocate us under the weight of public opinion. Against this, is our intense individualism, which "lodges in the very depths of each man's mind and heart that indefinable feeling, the instinctive inclination for political independence, and thus prepares the remedy for the ill which it engenders."[2]

We are used to internal tension; it's the very essence of American character. The system works wonderfully so long as we maintain our sense of balance, and remain engaged in both the creation of new wealth and the limitation of the powers of the state. Trouble sets in when we go overboard in the pursuit of personal satisfaction, forgetting about the common good. Dropping our vigilance on the appetites of ourselves and our rulers, we throw open the door to tyranny:

The discharge of political duties appears to them to be a troublesome impediment which diverts them from their occupations and business. If they are required to elect representatives, to support the government by personal service, to meet on public business, they think they have no time, they cannot waste their precious hours in useless engagements . . . These people think they are following the principle of self-interest, but the idea they entertain of that principle is a very crude one; and the better to look after what they call their own business, they neglect their chief business, which is to remain their own masters.[3]

Liberty cannot be divided into neat compartments. We cannot pretend to have freedom to pursue our own affairs at the same time we abandon the fight for our public freedoms. It is all or nothing. If we lose freedom in one area, it threatens all the others. The more we ask our rulers to exercise fundamental control over certain aspects of our lives, the more they will seek to gain control over all our other activities.

The first fatal step on the road to tyranny is self-indulgence, and the consequent abandonment of our collective national mission. Once we have committed all our energies to our personal satisfaction, we no longer sacrifice time and wealth to the free associations that shelter us from the appetites of the state. Politics, like nature, abhors a vacuum, and the government moves into the space we have abandoned, expanding its powers as we limit ours.

It's time to look more closely at the Faustian deal we first encountered in chapter 3: our rulers promise us material success, if only we leave them free to manage the society. Let us take care of everything, they say, and we'll make you rich and happy. The essence of the deal was perfectly embodied in Bill Clinton's reaction to the emergence of a budget surplus in the late 1990s. When someone suggested that the money should be returned to the taxpayers, he quickly replied, in a rare moment of candor, "they wouldn't know how to spend it. We will spend it better."

There was no public outcry at Clinton's ominous remark, for precisely the reason Tocqueville gives: we were in the midst of the greatest uninterrupted boom in our history, and we didn't want to do anything that might jeopardize it. Whatever his defects might have been, we were inclined to let our president do whatever he wanted. "If he attends for some time only to the material prosperity of the country," Tocqueville writes, in one of his most frighteningly accurate predictions of the ease with which a leader can amass power in a democratic society, "no more will be demanded of him."

It's an exaggeration, and Tocqueville immediately adds the corrective aside. Material prosperity isn't the only thing; there is also law and order. Even the wealthiest and self-sufficient people will vote out a government that has permitted the streets to become dangerous. "Men who are possessed by the passion for physical gratification generally find out that the turmoil of freedom disturbs their welfare before they discover how freedom itself serves to promote it . . ." Finishing the aside, Tocqueville acidly remarks that although it is certainly wonderful to have safe cities, "all nations have been enslaved by being kept in good order." If he had to choose between the turmoil of freedom and the tranquility of tyranny, Tocqueville would take his chances with turmoil, but most people go for tranquility. We'll sacrifice a lot of freedom in order to feel secure.

Stanley Kubrick's masterpiece *A Clockwork Orange* is perhaps the greatest cinematic rendering of this universal principle. We watch in horror as gangs of young hoodlums spread mayhem in their city, and then see the protagonist rendered incapable of violence by being conditioned to get sick whenever he thinks of committing a violent act. At first there is relief that his marauding days are over, but we gradually see, again to our horror, that he has been stripped of all freedom and has become a pathetic automaton.

Violent social unrest has provided the justification for many a modern dictatorship, from Mussolini in Italy to Fujimori in Peru and the generals in Turkey and Chile, while other authoritarian regimes have come to power against the backdrop of war, or the threat of war, as in Pakistan in the autumn of 1999. Emergency powers are invoked in the midst of the crisis, and remain in place long after the excuse has passed. We are rarely inclined to limit the powers of a government—even when it is politically possible—that has saved us from a crisis, whether it be terrorism or a great depression. We are very far from tyranny, but the expansion of the American government has followed the same course. The small, strictly limited government created by the Constitution has relentlessly expanded with our national crises, most notably after each of the three world wars of the twentieth century and during the depression of the 1930s.

Most of us imagine the transformation of a free society to a tyrannical state in Hollywood terms, as a melodramatic act of violence like a military coup or an armed insurrection. Not Tocqueville, who understands the process like a master surgeon excising a nasty malignancy. He foresees a slow death of freedom. The power of the centralized government will gradually expand, meddling in every area of our lives until, like a lobster in a slowly heated pot, we are cooked without ever realizing what has happened. Indeed, the ultimate horror of Tocqueville's vision is that we will welcome it, and even convince ourselves that we control it.

There is no single dramatic event in Tocqueville's scenario, no storming of the Bastille, no assault on the Winter Palace, no March on Rome, no Kristallnacht. We are to be immobilized, Gulliver-like, by myriad rules and regulations, annoying little restrictions that become more and more binding until they eventually paralyze us.

> Subjection in minor affairs breaks out every day and is felt by the whole community indiscriminately. It does not drive men to resistance, but it crosses them at every turn, till they are led to surrender the exercise of their own will. Thus their spirit is gradually broken and their character enervated . . . [4]

The tyranny he foresees for us does not have much in common with the vicious dictatorships of modern times. He apologizes for lacking the proper words with which to define it. He hesitates to call it either tyranny or despotism (although, lacking any better words, he uses the old ones), because it does not rule by terror or oppression. There are no secret police, no concentration camps, and no torture. "The nature of despotic power in democratic ages is not to be fierce or cruel, but minute and meddling."[5] The vision and even the language anticipate Orwell's *1984*, although *Democracy in America* was written more than a century earlier. Tocqueville describes the new tyranny as "an immense and tutelary power," and its task is to watch over us all, and regulate every aspect of our lives. "It covers the surface of society with a network of small complicated rules, minute and uniform, through which the most original minds and the most energetic characters cannot penetrate, to rise above the crowd."[6] Not, then, a mean-spirited dictatorship that crushes our individualism and kills anyone who challenges the authority of the ruler. Tocqueville is not talking about Hitler, Mao, or Stalin. We will not be bludgeoned into submission; we will be seduced. He foresees the collapse of American democracy as the end result of two parallel developments that ultimately render us meekly subservient to an enlarged bureaucratic power: the corruption of our character, and the emergence of a vast welfare state that manages all the details of our lives.

> That power is absolute, minute, regular, provident and mild. It would be like the authority of a parent if, like that authority, its object was to prepare men for manhood; but it seeks, on the contrary, to keep them in perpetual childhood: it is well content that the people should rejoice, provided they think of nothing but rejoicing. For their happiness such a government willingly labors, but it chooses to be the sole agent and the only arbiter of that happiness; it provides for their security, foresees and supplies

their necessities, facilitates their pleasures, manages their principal concerns, directs their industry, regulates the descent of property, and subdivides their inheritances: what remains, but to spare them all the care of thinking and all the trouble of living?

The metaphor of a parent maintaining perpetual control over his child is particularly prescient, for it is the language of American politics in the late 1990s. All manner of new governmental powers were justified in the name of "the children," from enhanced regulation of communications on the Internet to special punishments for "hate speech"; from the empowerment of social service institutions to crack down on parents who try to discipline their children, to the mammoth expansion of sexual quotas from university athletic programs to private businesses. Tocqueville particularly abhors such new governmental powers because they are federal, emanating from Washington, not from local governments. He reminds us that when the central government asserts its authority over states and communities, a tyrannical shadow is lurking just behind. So long as local governments are strong, he says, even tyrannical laws can be mitigated by moderate enforcement at the local level, but once the central government takes control of the entire structure, our liberties are at grave risk. When prosecutors invoke new federal laws to punish hoodlums who use guns near a school, instead of using state legislation that already bans the weapons, we should resist it as an unwarranted expansion of the central government. People who are serious about defending their freedom must seek to accomplish their objectives by themselves whenever possible.

It is evident that our associations, along with religion one of the two keys to the great success of the American experiment, are prime targets for the appetite of the state. In the seamless web created by the new tyranny, everything from the Boy Scouts to smoking clubs will be strictly regulated. It is no accident that the campaign to drive religion out of American public life began in the 1940s, when the government was consolidating its unprecedented expansion during the depression and the Second World War, having asserted its control over a wide range of activities that had previously been entrusted to the judgment of private groups and individuals.

When we console ourselves with the thought that the government is, after all, doing it for a good reason and to accomplish a worthy objective, we unwittingly turn up the temperature under our lobster-pot. The road to the Faustian deal is paved with the finest intentions, but the last stop is the ruin of our soul. Permitting the central government to assume our proper responsibilities is not merely a transfer of power from us to them; it does grave damage to our spirit. It subverts our national character. In Tocqueville's elegant construction, it "renders the exercise of the free agency of man less useful and less frequent; it circumscribes the will within a narrower range and gradually robs a man of all the uses of himself." We are brought to heel slowly and gently. Just as he warned us earlier, once we go over the edge toward the pursuit of material wealth, our energies uncoil, and we become meek, quiescent and flaccid in the defense of freedom.

> The will of man is not shattered, but softened, bent, and guided; men are seldom forced by it to act, but they are constantly restrained from acting. Such a power does not destroy, but it prevents existence; it does not tyrannize, but it compresses, enervates, extinguishes, and stupefies a people, till each nation is reduced to nothing better than a flock of timid and industrious animals, of which the government is the shepherd.

The devilish genius of this form of tyranny is that it looks and even acts democratic. We still elect our representatives, and they still ask us for our support. ". . . servitude of the regular, quiet, and gentle kind . . . might be combined with some of the outward forms of freedom, and . . . might even establish itself under the wing of the sovereignty of the people." Freedom is smothered without touching the institutions of political democracy. We play a terrible joke on ourselves, acting out democratic skits while submitting to an oppressive central power that we ourselves have chosen. "They devise a sole, tutelary and all-powerful form of government, but elected by the people . . . this gives them a respite: they console themselves for being in tutelage by the reflection that they have chosen their own guardians."[7]

There is a very old joke about the husband who announces that he has a perfect marriage: he makes all the big decisions, and lets his wife deal with the minor matters. He decides when the country should go to war, while she manages the family budget. He decides who should govern America, and she makes all the decisions about the upbringing of the children: where they go to school, what they wear, how much allowance they receive, and so on. That is precisely the sort of division of powers Tocqueville fears for us. We will be permitted to make the big decisions: who will be president, and who will sit in the legislature. But it will not matter, because the state will decide how our money will be spent, how our children will be raised, and how we will behave, down to the details of the language we are permitted to use.

We laugh at the joke because we realize that the husband's "big decisions" are meaningless; the same eventually applies to a "democratic" state that makes all our little decisions for us. Tocqueville unerringly puts his finger on the absurdity: We give power to the state in matters that require only simple good sense, as if we were incapable of exercising it. But we elect the government itself, as if we were the very incarnation of wisdom. We are "alternately made the playthings of [our] ruler, and his masters, more than kings and less than men."[8]

We may chuckle, but it is the rueful laugh of the powerless, because such a government is far harder to resist than a traditional tyranny. "Nothing is so irresistible as a tyrannical power commanding in the name of the people," Tocqueville intones, because it wields the awesome moral power of the majority and "acts . . . with the quickness and the persistence of a single man."[9]

As Tocqueville grimly predicted, modern totalitarians have thoroughly mastered this lesson. Nazis, Fascists, and Communists have passionately preached sermons of equality, and constantly paid formal homage to the sovereignty of the people. Hitler proclaimed himself *primus inter pares*, the first among equals, while Mao and Stalin claimed their authority in the name of a classless society where everyone would be equal. And, while Communism was brought to power by violent coups, Fascism was not installed by violence. Hitler and Mussolini were popular leaders, their authority was sanctioned by great electoral victories and repeated demonstrations of mass public enthusiasm, and neither of them was ever challenged by a significant percentage of the population. The great Israeli historian Jacob Talmon coined the perfect name for this perversion of the Enlightenment dream, which enslaves all in the name of all: totalitarian democracy.[10]

These extreme cases help us understand Tocqueville's brilliant warning that equality is not a defense against tyranny, but an open invitation to ambitious and cunning leaders who enlist our support in depriving ourselves of freedom. He summarizes it in two sentences that should be memorized by every American who cherishes freedom:

The . . . sole condition required in order to succeed in centralizing the supreme power in a democratic community is to love equality, or to get men to believe you love it. Thus the science of despotism, which was once so complex, is simplified, and reduced, as it were, to a single principle.[11]

## THE CORRUPTION OF AMERICAN CHARACTER

Each advance in the powers of government, each surrender of an additional quantum of our freedom, represents a corruption of our basic character, yet there are times when it is the lesser of ineluctable evils. We needed a big, powerful government to wage the three world wars of the twentieth century and cope with the Great Depression, and survival trumps individualism every time. Once in place, the big government followed its preordained path, and sought to expand.

If we were ever faced with a choice between individualism and the kind of coddling mama-state Tocqueville dreads, we would draw a line and fight for our freedoms (the public opinion polls are unmistakably clear), but we never had the luxury of such a "moment of truth." The biggest changes were taken in highly charged moments, and presented by national heroes who stigmatized their criticis as greedy and uncaring people. Franklin Delano Roosevelt's famous campaign address in Madison Square Garden in 1936, when he spoke of the boom of the 1920s and the 1929 crash that led to his election in 1932, is a classic example. "Nine wild years of the golden calf, and three long years of the scourge. Nine frantic years at the ticker, and three hard years in the breadlines . . ." The New Deal wasn't merely a rescue operation for the broke, the hungry, and the unemployed; like all our great national enterprises, it was presented as a crusade against evil itself. When Lyndon Johnson proposed the Great Society legislation of the mid-1960s he evoked similar themes, presenting his program as a moral necessity. Each change was viewed as a single decision, not part of a pattern, and as Tocqueville predicted, we grew accustomed to it. We even liked it.

Political leaders rarely have the courage to underline the loss of freedom that we suffer by permitting the central government to expand, even for the most admirable reasons. It takes a Davy Crockett to remind us of our responsibilities. When he was in Congress, Crockett challenged the authority of the government to pay for the restoration of housing in downtown Washington, D.C., that had been destroyed in a fire. Crockett was all in favor of rebuilding the gutted homes, but he thought he had a better way to pay for it. Instead of spending the taxpayers' money, he called upon his fellow representatives to contribute a month's salary to this worthy cause, and offered to be the first donor. Like Tocqueville, this frontier hero had a visceral distrust of government actions, and he also understood the importance of every citizen bearing an active share of the common burden. If it's our money anyway, he reasoned, why funnel it through the government?

Tocqueville is certainly not opposed to safety nets for the poor, job security for workers, or medical treatment for the ill. He cares every bit as much as the most fervent advocate of the welfare state. But he also cares about freedom, and he knows that every time we ask the central government to address a problem we pay a political and spiritual price, and invite even greater intrusions in our daily lives. Every time the bureaucracy tackles a new problem, it deprives us of the opportunity, thereby undermining our character. If we do it often enough, we will turn into the meek little sheep of Tocqueville's vision.

Tocqueville insists that to maintain our unique character we must limit our pursuit of personal success and devote a good part of our energies to working for the common good. We must maintain our moral compass, constantly reminding ourselves, as he neatly puts it, that there is an intimate connection "between the private fortune of each and the prosperity of all."[12] We have to keep the channels of upward and downward mobility wide open, as our fathers taught us: it is one of the building blocks of the American dream.

It is much harder to do it ourselves than to have the government do it for us, even though we know that we should act, and that the governmental "solution" is not only less efficient than the private one, but a source of still more problems. Knowing this, we feel guilty at each concession of power to the government, and we need soothing rationalizations for our inaction, less we look in our national mirror and see black marks of corruption spreading over us. We've used several excuses, and Tocqueville is quick to spot them. The first, one of our national favorites, is the pretense that history is guided by enormous forces over which we have little or no control. Although all our experience shows that a handful of determined men, or even a single courageous individual, can transform the world, we are tempted by theories of history and society that swamp individual effort by arguing that great events are produced by vast, impersonal forces. We like these big theories, because they save us the intellectual labor of digging deeply into the facts and going through the hard work of analyzing them correctly, and they also absolve us of responsibility for our own problems. Who can blame us if we are simply the victims of forces far more powerful than ourselves? We hardly need to be reminded of the dangers of thinking of ourselves as victims, or of its seductive allure in late twentieth-century America, where victimhood has become an eagerly pursued and often surprisingly well-rewarded status.

Tocqueville is disturbed by the success of "big theories" in the United States, whether they be sociological theories that purport to explain the latest crisis, or nutritional theories that promise to make us all thin without having to work at it, or new historical models that tell us what is going to happen next. In the 1990s we were entranced by theories of "economic overreach" that purported to explain why the Soviet Union and Japan were more stable and successful than the United States, other theories that predicted why, after the Cold War, economic power would be more important than military might, and still more theories predicting the imminent obsolescence of the nation-state, doomed to extinction by the latest megatrend.

Tocqueville does not believe in big historical theories, and despises those who advance them. A big theory, he haughtily proclaims, "indulges the indolence or incapacity of their minds while it confers upon them the honors of deep thinking."[13] He knows that most historical events are the result of individual decisions and actions, along with luck, not the outcome of the movement of vast forces.

The worst thing about such theories is political and psychological: they paralyze us, for the same reason they absolve us of responsibility. If everything is predetermined, why bother to do anything? It's all going to happen anyway. We might as well tend to our garden, because we don't matter. The "forces of history" will decide the outcome.

It's just what any ambitious would-be tyrant would want us to think.

The second great rationalization for inaction is cynicism, the bitter conviction that the system is corrupt, and that virtue cannot possibly prevail. Tocqueville agrees that the charge is serious. He has seen abundant corruption in America, (even though he insists we are the most ethical people he has encountered), and he believes it is an inescapable element of any democratic system. How could it be otherwise? In an egalitarian society that opens political advancement to all, people from modest backgrounds often rise to high positions. Tocqueville pointedly observes that such persons still have to make their fortunes. Men on the make are famously corruptible, and there is never a shortage of corruptors. According to the *Wall Street Journal*, California state officials have had to send monitors to San Francisco on election day at least three times between 1995 and 1999 because of electoral "irregularities" and "disarray and confusion." A Pennsylvania state senator was thrown out of office because of fraud in 1994 and sixteen people were either convicted or pleaded guilty of absentee ballot fraud.[14] We have a long-standing tradition of electing impeached or convicted public officials to high office, from Adam Clayton

Powell and Alcee Hastings in Congress to Marion Barry,
the oft-elected former mayor of Washington, D.C., and
his notorious role model, Boss Hague of Jersey City.

Tocqueville is certainly not shocked by our corruption
(who ever heard of a Frenchman shocked by the spectacle of corruption?), but he is more concerned about it
here than in more traditional societies. In Europe, rich
and powerful political leaders seek to buy the support of
the lower classes, thereby engaging in a single corrupt
act whose effects are likely to be short lived. In America,
since the rich and powerful tend to be in business rather
than government, they corrupt the leaders, trading financial favors for political ones. Sometimes the two are
combined, although rarely in the same generation (in
1960, for example, Kennedy family money helped elect
John Kennedy president, as when the dead voted in record numbers in Cook County, Illinois). In this manner,
the politicians' success becomes associated in the public
mind with "low intrigues and immoral practices,"
thereby producing a paralyzing cynicism.

As the rulers of democratic nations are almost always suspected of dishonorable conduct, they in
some measure lend the authority of the government
to the base practices of which they are accused.
They thus afford dangerous examples, which dis-

courage the struggle of virtuous independence and
cloak with authority the secret designs of wickedness . . . The corruption of men who have casually
risen to power has a coarse and vulgar infection in
it that renders it dangerous to the multitude.[15]

Like all great political thinkers, Tocqueville understands that a free society can survive corrupt leaders, so
long as the corruption is limited to the elites. He even
lapses into a half-hearted defense of corrupt aristocrats
by musing that the corruption of great men has "a certain
grandeur." Freedom can be preserved if the people remain virtuous, and we are fortunate that our best people—those who must emerge to lead us at moments of
crisis—do not usually go into politics in the first place,
and are thus shielded from direct corruption. But this bit
of luck cannot last forever. If not rooted out, corruption
eventually spreads, destroys the virtue of the people, and
undermines the legitimacy of the government. Once that
point is reached, we are easy prey for ambitious men
who want to dominate us.

The poison of corruption enters our souls through two
parallel channels.

First, as Tocqueville has just warned us, the spectacle
of corrupt leadership justifies corruption at all other lev-
els. The great and the abominable both lead by example,

because both virtue and wickedness attract. Bill Clinton well understood this when he permitted his spokesmen to explain away his sins by whispering "everybody does it." Like any good self-fulfilling prophecy, Clinton's preferred transgressions spread rapidly: oral sex became the diversion of choice for adolescents, and attorneys found increasing numbers of clients willing to lie to judges and juries about charges of sexual harassment.

The spectacle of corrupt leaders has a second devastating consequence: it convinces us that one cannot arrive at the top of the political heap by behaving ethically. For Tocqueville, this is the most devastating effect of all, because it destroys the legitimacy of government itself.

What is to be feared is not so much the immorality of the great as the fact that immorality may lead to greatness . . . [the people] are led to inquire how the person who was yesterday their equal is today their ruler . . . They are therefore led, and often rightly, to impute his success mainly to some of his vices; and an odious connection is thus formed between the ideas of turpitude and power, unworthiness and success, utility and dishonor.[16]

Once the public believes that our leaders have reached their high positions because they are corrupt, the government loses legitimacy. Under such a corrupt system, freedom is crushed, even if the rulers are formally designated by elections. As Tocqueville says, we become less than men and more than kings; less than men, because we are powerless against the dictates of our rulers, and more than kings because we still choose among them.

Tocqueville has in mind the kind of base corruption we typically associate with old-fashioned city mobs, like the Pendergasts in Kansas City, or Mayor Frank Hague of Jersey City, or Mayor Marion Barry in Washington, D.C. Tax money is used to pay off friends of the government instead of funding worthy projects, top officials get kickbacks, and fair competition is replaced by cronyism. If you want to get ahead, you'd better join the mob.

Call it Mafia politics. This is not a subtle, hidden corruption, but an arrogant and aggressive intrusion into both business and politics, to their mutual ruin. There is no mistaking the symptoms of this process; even the most unsophisticated citizen sees what is going on.

The people can never penetrate into the dark labyrinth of court intrigue, and will always have difficulty in detecting the turpitude that lurks under delicate manners, refined tastes, and graceful language. But to pillage the public purse and to sell the favors of the state are arts that the meanest villain can understand and hope to practice in his turn.

## CLINTON: A NEW FORM OF CORRUPTION

We are certainly not immune to Mafia politics, and while it has usually been limited to local governments, we have occasionally had it at the highest level, as in the Teapot Dome scandal in the roaring twenties. A 1999 study of international corruption by Transparency International gave the United States a score of 7.5 out of a perfect ten, behind Denmark (10), Singapore (9.1), and Germany (8).[17] This is not the sort of score that Tocqueville anticipates from people he describes as incessantly vigilant over the slightest sign of moral turpitude.

Worst of all, in the 1990s we saw, for the first time in our history, a president willing to accept political favors from potentially hostile foreign powers, at the same time he took extraordinary steps to make them more powerful. Even more ominously, Bill Clinton not only enabled the People's Republic of China to obtain our finest military technology while accepting contributions to his political campaigns; whenever professional civil servants charged with guarding our national security challenged his actions, they were intimidated by their political superiors.

During the Reagan years we crafted an international system to prevent dangerous technology from going to dangerous countries. This required an enormous input from professional civil servants, particularly in the military, to evaluate the impact of high tech sales to actual and potential enemies. It would have been unthinkable for those experts to have been successfully silenced or coerced into lying about matters that directly affected the survival of the nation. This happened repeatedly during the Clinton years, hand in hand with the systematic dismantling of the system to safeguard our military superiority.

Shortly before Chinese premier Jiang Zemin's arrival in Washington in the fall of 1997 for his summit with Bill Clinton, the White House was pushing the State, Defense, and Energy Departments to support a presidential certification of China as a nuclear nonproliferator, and to sign off on the creation of an "information exchange and technical cooperative reciprocal arrangement" on ostensibly civilian nuclear technology. This "arrangement" would give the Chinese easy access to American civil reactor sites, provide them with detailed information on how the United States handles fissionable materials, and give them access to operational data on U.S. nuclear sites.

Despite the pressure from the White House, an attorney on the arms control staff of the Defense Special Weapons Agency, Mr. Jonathan Fox, wrote a memo that said, in no uncertain terms, that China *was* a nuclear proliferator, and that the proposed arrangement was "a technology transfer agreement swaddled in the comforting yet misleading terminology of a confidence-building measure." Fox's memo argued against the agreement on the grounds that:

- (it) presents real and substantial risk to the common defense and security of both the United States and allied countries;
- (it) can result in a significant increase of the risk of nuclear weapons technology proliferation;
- the environment surrounding these exchange measures cannot guarantee timely warning of willful diversion of otherwise confidential information to non-nuclear states for nuclear weapons development,
- there was no guarantee that the nuclear information would be limited to non-military applications in China itself.

Mr. Fox noted that China chafes at its inferiority to the West, and "now seeks to redress that balance through industrial, academic and military espionage. China routinely, both overtly and covertly, subverts national and multilateral trade controls on militarily critical items."

Issues of such enormous magnitude should have been resolved only after considerable discussion and debate, but the Clinton administration stifled all debate, and imposed its decision on the bureaucracy.

On October 24, 1997, Mr. Fox was called out of an interagency meeting to receive an urgent telephone call from a superior in the Office of Non-Proliferation Policy in the Department of Defense. Fox was told that unless he changed the memo and recommended in favor of the agreement, he could look elsewhere for employment.

Within an hour, all the critical language had been deleted, and the memo now simply concluded that the agreement "is not inimical to the common defense or the security of the United States." Worried that his earlier draft might fall into unfriendly hands (thereby providing a paper trail that would show he had altered his recommendation), his superiors insisted that somebody else sign the new memo.

The arrangement was consequently in place in time for the summit with the Chinese ruler, even though President Clinton and the entire American national security team knew full well that Fox had told the truth: China was spreading militarily useful nuclear technology among the rogue nations of Asia and the Middle East. Indeed, it was precisely this knowledge, and the fear that somebody in the media or the Congress might enunciate it at an embarrassing moment, that drove the Administration to silence potential truth-tellers.

Jonathan Fox is not the only weapons expert in the United States Government to have been instructed to lie or remain silent about the true consequences of sending military technology to China. Notra Trulock and his colleagues were told by their superiors at the Department of Energy that they should stop annoying people with accounts of Chinese espionage at Los Alamos, and other professionals in the Pentagon—some of whom, like Michael Maloof and Peter Leitner, spoke publicly—were told to shut up about the approval of hi-tech licenses that would inevitably strengthen Chinese military power. When they did not submit to the gag order, the experts' advice was simply falsified. On at least two occasions military experts who recommended against high-tech exports to China, later discovered that their recommendations had been altered in the Pentagon's computerized data base.

No government welcomes criticism, and elected officials are routinely annoyed by civil servants who try to tell them how to perform their jobs. The skill of bureaucratic manipulation of their political superiors has been immortalized in the hilarious British television comedies *Yes, Minister* and *Yes, Prime Minister*, but the Clinton administration's haughty dismissal of challenges to its China policy by experts within the American government is quite different. This issue could involve the very survival of the United States. To silence criticism on such matters is a folly verging on criminal irresponsibility, and it is particularly ominous against the background of years of secret Chinese political contributions to Bill Clinton. Bill Triplett and Ed Timperlake have shown that money from the Chinese military establishment rescued Clinton at several crucial moments in his political career.[18]

The combination of Chinese money to Clinton, and the president's policy of largesse to the Chinese, creates that "odious connection between turpitude and power" that can destroy our democratic enterprise. And just as Tocqueville feared, the reaction to the perversely intimate embrace between the American president and the Communist regime in China was muted, despite the unanimous finding of the bipartisan Cox Commission in Congress that our national security had been seriously compromised by sales to, and thefts of, advanced military technology by Communist China. There was no follow-up by major news organizations when the Fox network reported that there were FBI intercepts showing that the White House had coordinated its public statements on Chinese campaign financing with the regime in Beijing. There was no sustained investigation by Congress, even though it was controlled by the opposition Republican Party.

Tocqueville knew that we would eventually reach a potential turning point, when we would have to choose between blind pursuit of our personal satisfactions and a resolute defense of our freedom against an ever more powerful government that promised us greater wealth and greater happiness in exchange for greater power over our lives. He feared that we would make the wrong choice, but he insisted that it was a free one: if we lost our freedom, we would have no one to blame but ourselves. If we want to preserve our freedom, we're going to have to fight for it.

## THE WAY OUT

We are certainly not doomed. Tocqueville is talking about the dark side of our character to alert us to the dangers we carry within us, the better for us to resist and defeat them. He wants us to recognize that government will inevitably seek to extend its powers over us, so that we will resist it. When he insists that "individual independence and local liberties will ever be the products of art . . . centralization will be the natural government,"[19] he is calling on us to revive our national mission, to reassert our basic character against a corrupt government that is expanding its domination of us.

If we do not understand our peril, we will fall for the Faustian deal. That is why Tocqueville puts a proper education at the top of his requirements for a free man. He is pleased to find that Americans are extremely well educated. He even believes a prison warden who tells him that, during twenty years, he never encountered an inmate who could not read and write. Tocqueville tells us that throughout his travels, from the great cities to the most remote settlement on the frontier, he constantly found Americans fully informed about their own rights and the means to protect them (although woefully ignorant about foreign affairs). "In the United States," he concludes, "politics are the end and aim of education."[20]

Tocqueville immediately adds that education does not mean mere book learning, and he lambasts the intellectuals who claim that anyone can be made fit for democratic citizenship simply by becoming literate. "If the Americans had not been gradually accustomed to govern themselves, their book-learning would not help them much . . ." He admires us for our democratic experience, which, along with good education, provides us with good common sense. People of this timbre are hard to lead into servitude.

Would that we had maintained such high standards. No one believes that our children are well educated today, and rightly so: on top of our traditional ignorance of foreign languages, geography, and history, our scores on mathematics aptitude tests are in the bottom half of those in the industrialized world. You do not have to be a math whiz to know something is wrong when American computer companies beg Washington for higher immigrant quotas for skilled Asian programmers, and you do not need to have a Ph.D. in education to know why our schools are failing. They are increasingly being asked to replace parents.

The demand that school teachers teach values instead of reading, writing, and arithmetic, and the insistence that the classroom be a chorus of self-esteem instead of an example of the highest academic standards, is a further symptom of our lopsided self-indulgence. Just as our pursuit of wealth weakens our engagement in political and religious associations, so it also undermines our commitment to family life. We see further evidence in our high rates of divorce and illegitimacy and in their social consequences, juvenile crime and school dropouts. Once again, Tocqueville lays out the inevitable outcome: the government expands into schools and families, telling teachers how to raise our children (replacing parents in everything from sex education to ethics), and limiting our own ability to discipline our children, even encouraging the kids to sue us if we transgress by being overly strict. Earlier, we heard Tocqueville warn us that the "anything goes" doctrine "seems to have been invented in an age of freedom to shelter all future tyrants."[21] Here is yet another example of his prescience: the more our traditional moral standards are abandoned, the more powerful the government becomes.

Unlike the Americans Tocqueville encountered, our knowledge of the Constitution is shockingly poor, leaving us more easily manipulated by political hucksters who offer us new "rights" undreamt-of by the Founders. If the schools do not teach our children the fundamental elements of our free society, they can hardly be expected to defend it. They will follow in our footsteps, accept the government's "feel good" options, and move further into the arms of the fatal Faustian deal.

We have plenty of work to do, which is as it should be. Leaving Constitution Hall in Philadelphia, Benjamin Franklin summed it up in a single phrase when asked what form of government he and the other Founders had created. "A republic," he replied, "if you know how to keep it." It was always up to us.

Tocqueville has some advice.

- Above all, he says, reject the government's offer of expanded comfort. Do it yourselves, through the associations that have made us the envy of the world;
- Don't believe the intellectuals who try to convince us that everything is part of a vast, preordained pattern. It is not so. Most of the time, success is the result of virtuous hard work and hard thinking, and failure is earned by inattention and self-indulgence. We have the right character based on the right values, and we must insist that our leaders respect them;
- The most important quality in a leader is farsightedness. The road to corruption begins with an obsession with personal short-term gain, while the path to virtue is long, passing through many generations toward a distant paradise;
- Do not tolerate Mafia politics; root out corruption whenever it appears, remembering Tocqueville's dictum:

The sudden and undeserved promotion of a courtier produces only a transient impression in an aristocratic country . . . But nothing is more pernicious than similar instances of favor exhibited to a democratic people . . . no greatness should be of too easy acquirement and . . . ambition should be obliged to fix its gaze long upon an object before it is gratified[22];

- Beware those who seek to banish religion from all sectors of public life, remembering that we separated church and state in order to protect religion, not to secularize the society. Tocqueville believes religion to be the best remedy for self-indulgence, and the most secure defender of our liberty. If we follow our instincts we will surely prevail, and the twenty-first century will take us even closer to the fulfillment of our national mission. If, instead, we listen to the siren song of the Faustian deal, we will pass into history as yet another example of a great civilization that lost its inner fortitude, and thus its glory.

At least it will have been a free choice.

# CONCLUSION

———◆———

## MORE TOCQUEVILLIAN THAN EVER BEFORE

*Life is not a pleasure, nor a misery, but a serious undertaking with which we are charged and which must be conducted and ended to our honor.*

No one before or since has understood us so well as Alexis de Tocqueville, and no one can be considered an educated person without having grappled with Tocqueville's profound inquiry into American character. Tocqueville knew that the destiny of half the world would eventually depend upon Americans, and it behooves everyone involved in that adventure—Americans and foreigners, friends and foes—to listen closely.

The world risks pneumonia if the United States sneezes, and Tocqueville is our master diagnostician.

Tocqueville knows that we are a bundle of contradictions, and our inner turmoil is the source of our amazing energy. We are simultaneously and passionately religious and secular, isolationist and interventionist, pragmatic and idealistic, legalistic and iconoclastic. We even have tensions within tensions: our versions of Protestantism invariably stress the redeeming value of work and wealth at the same time they warn against the corrupting force of great material luxury. Anyone who tries to slap a simple label on us has missed the whole point.

Above all, we are revolutionaries. Like Jim Clyman, the mountain man who spent his years crisscrossing the frontier, building up the fur trade, befriending or fighting friendly or hostile Indians, guiding new emigrants across the continent to the Pacific Coast, and finally settling down to live out his allotted time in Napa Valley, California, we change whatever we touch. Sometimes we do it deliberately, sometimes we just do it, but Americans never leave things the way they found them. We are dreamers and world-shapers, and in fairly short order we will reshape the heavens as well. Neil Armstrong was only the first of many yet to come.

We didn't need Karl Marx to tell us that while the philosophers had sought to understand the world, the point is to change it; we are the most potent engine of change in human history, always tearing down old ideas and institutions, buildings, and bridges, to build newer ones. Creative destruction is our middle name, it is our second nature. In our hands, even the seemingly mundane process of manufacturing becomes a revolutionary process. Listen to the story of that most American piece of hardware, the Colt handgun.

From 1836 to 1842 Samuel Colt had manufactured about five or six thousand of his patent revolvers, the first successful repeating firearms. It was a technological master stroke, but a financial flop, and Colt had to shut down the factory. Nonetheless, the guns became the weapon of choice of American fighters and pioneers, from the Texas Rangers and Kit Carson to the traders in Santa Fe. They knew the Colt was the most effective weapon against the formidable Plains Indians—by far the most menacing to the explorers and emigrants headed West. As DeVoto tells us, "nearly all of the primordial five or six thousand had, by 1846, gravitated to the place where they were needed, the Western frontier . . . nearly every writer who discusses outfits for emigrants recommends them."[1]

It was indeed the gun that conquered the West.

So great was the fame of Colt's revolvers that in 1846 the War Department demanded that he go back to work in order to supply American forces fighting Mexicans in Texas. He'd lost his original plans and had to redesign the pistol from memory, but this was easily accomplished, and Colt set up shop outside New Haven, Connecticut, in a joint venture with the son of Eli Whitney, the inventor of the cotton gin. Together they designed new machine tools, and dramatically improved the efficiency of the process. It is a measure of the American passion for change that, while there were many manual operations in Colt's original factory, by 1846 virtually the entire process had been mechanized on an assembly line. Nothing better exemplifies our revolutionary nature than Samuel Colt's new manufacturing methods: as the product was improved, it became simpler, economies of scale were realized so it became more affordable, and the Colt soon dominated the world market.

The pattern of this typical American success story is imbedded in our national genetic code, for it recurs in every generation. Henry Ford, Thomas Alva Edison, Levi Strauss, Steve Jobs, and countless others were forged from the same mold. Colt and Whitney not only revolutionized America, they transformed the entire industrial universe. Their new machine tools were so advanced that when Colt went to build a factory in England a few years later, he could not find local laborers skilled enough to work for him, or any English or European machinery with the necessary precision. Workers and machine tools had to be shipped across the Atlantic from America. Barely twenty years earlier, New England textile manufacturers had to smuggle English machine tools into Massachusetts to produce the highest quality textiles. Colt and Whitney reversed the flow of advanced technology in less than a generation. In Tocqueville's time American inventions established the world standard in everything from the finest steel to the fastest sailing ships, from the cotton gin to the most efficient printing press.

The misguided intellectuals, who in the late 1980s announced that America had fallen hopelessly behind Japan and Germany in the manufacture of everything from computers to automobiles, had forgotten one of Tocqueville's basic insights into our national character: we love a good challenge, and we can rethink, retool, and restructure faster than anybody else. The Germans and the Japanese now look to us for inspiration, and they manufacture a large percentage of their automobiles here in America.

We should not be surprised at this all too familiar intellectual blunder; we have long had an embittered intelligentsia in America, jealous of their European counterparts and contemptuous of their own fellow-citizens, because Americans do not esteem intellectuals as the Europeans do. Angry at our failure to raise them to the heights they believe they deserve, a surprising number of American intellectuals have underestimated the strength and wisdom of our basic character, not least of all our deep religious convictions.

Tocqueville knows that just beneath our drive for material success lies a hard core of religious faith that anchors all our activities. We are a frenetic people with a messianic vision of achieving happiness and goodness, first for ourselves, then for all mankind, and we are always in danger of losing our balance between the drive for personal satisfaction and the necessity of collective action to advance the common good. Religion constantly reminds us that we need to resist personal temptation, and to address the needs of the less fortunate. Religion lies at the very heart of the American enterprise, for without the morality that religion imposes, we risk a rapid descent into a frenzied pursuit of personal satisfaction. Tocqueville believes that if we were ever to lose our religious convictions, our fall would have two deadly consequences:

- first, having escaped the tension between the quest for personal success and the moral requirements of our faith, we would lose our unique energy (in his elegant metaphor, we would "uncoil");
- second, having discarded our commitment to the common good, we would fall prey to ambitious tyrants.

Tocqueville does not think it is very likely that we will lose our religious moorings, despite the concerted efforts of radical secularists. Unlike many contemporary intellectuals, he knows (and knows the reason why) the separation of church and state was not supposed to drive religion out of public life, but was instead intended to protect religion from the predations of the government. Tocqueville hails it for that reason.

Nonetheless, Tocqueville foresees the risk of tyranny in America, and he constantly warns us that we have far too few safeguards to protect our liberty. Indeed, one form of tyranny is part and parcel of our character: the tyranny of the majority that is implicit in our radical egalitarianism. Originality and individual creativity are throttled by standards imposed by majority convictions, and he is so impressed with the power of the American majority that he goes so far as to proclaim the absence of freedom of expression. Although he coins the term "individualism" during his brilliant exploration of the United States, and is a great admirer of our frontier spirit, he also sees the enormous pressure for conformity that we exert on ourselves.

Looking into the future, he tries to imagine the contours of an American-style tyranny, and how it might take shape. A revolutionary people will not fall victim to a tyranny of the traditional sort, and he does not believe that we will be taken over by an oppressor set on crushing our liberties. Rather, he believes that if we fall, we will be the victims of our own fatal shortcomings.

In Tocqueville's nightmare vision we will devote all our energies to the pursuit of personal enrichment and satisfaction, abandoning the free associations that have thus far protected us from a powerful central government, and asking our rulers to assume new responsibilities and to exert new powers. Knowing full well that every government automatically seeks to expand its power, Tocqueville warns that if we ask government to do things that we should be doing ourselves, we seal our own fate. He implores us to remain true to our basic character, and unite to advance the common good.

Our contemporaries are only too prone to doubt of human free will, because each of them feels himself confined on every side by his own weakness; but they are still willing to acknowledge the strength and independence of men united in society. Do not let this principle be lost sight of, *for the great object in our time is to raise the faculties of men, not to complete their prostration* [emphasis added].[2]

Tocqueville is not by nature an optimist, but he cannot help being inspired by the spectacle of Americans conquering a continent, dominating the native inhabitants, enriching themselves and expanding their numbers, creating a new form of government, inventing new methods of commerce, agriculture, industry and transportation, and doing it all with an amazing and seemingly impossible combination of radical individualism and radical egalitarianism. Neither he nor anyone else has ever seen anything quite like us, and he desperately hopes we will keep it up, balance equality against freedom, and eventually transform the whole world.

Anyone looking cold bloodedly at human history would bet against us. But then, according to all the odds, we shouldn't have gotten this far. The best news about our future is that it's still in our own strong hands.

# ACKNOWLEDGMENTS

The idea for this book wasn't mine; it was Mac Talley's. In this day and age it's almost impossible to find a great editor, and I'm grateful that Truman Talley wants me to write for him.

I am one of those fortunate souls who work at the American Enterprise Institute, and my thanks go to Chris DeMuth, our president, and David Gerson, our vice president, as well as to my friends and colleagues Walter Berns, Robert Bork, Michael Novak, Norman Ornstein, Irving Kristol, and David Wurmser, who read early drafts or discussed Tocqueville with me. They helped eliminate some errors, as did Professor Walter Dean Burnham of the University of Texas, at Austin. Irving Louis Horowitz told me I couldn't write this book without reading Bernard DeVoto, and as usual he was right. Everybody should read *The Year of Decision: 1846*. Maybe we'd start writing good popular history again. A long-term thank you to Richard Heffner, who first taught me the glories and subtleties of Alexis de Tocqueville at the New School for Social Research during the Kennedy-

Nixon campaign, and whose edition of *Democracy in America* is still the best short version.

As always, my gratitude to those generous people who support the Freedom Chair. I hope they enjoy this literary dividend.

Special thanks to Lynn Chu and Glen Hartley, my wonderful literary agents.

Annalisa Sheelar, Francesco Meucci, and Adam Storch did a lot of the research, and Annalisa managed the production of the manuscript.

It's always an ordeal for my family, but they're getting more patient with me. Simone now has her own career to worry about and was saved the worst of this project, but even Gabe, who was busy applying to college, and Daniel, preparing for Bar Mitzvah, took it with good humor. It seems impossible, but Barbara Ledeen is more wonderful with every passing year.

This book is dedicated to the memory of Grandma Mashe Levine, who explained politics to me when I was very young and she was, or at least seemed, very old. "Best government," she said, "good Czar. Worst government, bad Czar. More bad Czars than good Czars."

Tocqueville agrees.

# NOTES

---◆---

## INTRODUCTION:
### RESTLESS PEOPLE INSPIRED BY IDEAS, FOREVER HEADED FOR NEW FRONTIERS

1. Bernard DeVoto, *The Year of Decision: 1846* (Boston: Houghton Mifflin, 1943), p. 58.
2. Quoted in DeVoto, *The Year of Decision: 1846*, p. 53.
3. Alexis de Tocqueville, *Democracy in America*, ed. Phillips Bradley, vol. 1 (New York: Alfred A. Knopf, 1972), pp. 31–32.
4. Tocqueville, *Quinze Jours au Désert*, quoted in George Wilson Pierson, *Tocqueville in America* (Baltimore: Johns Hopkins University Press, 1996), p. 245.
5. Quoted in Pierson, *Tocqueville in America*, pp. 568–69.
6. Ibid., p. 235.
7. Pierson, *Tocqueville in America*, p. 609.

## CHAPTER 1:
### DYNAMIC PEOPLE DRIVEN BY INTERNAL CONFLICTS

1. Tocqueville, *Democracy in America*, vol. 1, p. 1.
2. Ibid., p. 52.
3. Ibid., p. 295.
4. Tocqueville, *Democracy in America*, vol. 2, p. 237.
5. *Washington Times National Weekly Edition*, 8–14 June 1998.
6. Tocqueville, *Democracy in America*, vol. 1, p. 289.
7. Ibid., p. 200.

8. Ibid., p. 53.
9. Everett Carl Ladd, *The Ladd Report* (New York: Free Press, 1999), p. 111.
10. Ibid, p. 118.
11. Luigi Barzini, *O America* (New York: Harper & Row, 1977), pp. 234–235.
12. Quoted in David R. Henderson, review of Dwight R. Lee and Richard B. McKenzie, *Getting Rich in America*, in *Milken Institute Review* (Third Quarter, 1999): 81.
13. hwww.issues-views.com./without commerce.sht
14. Bernard Wysocki Jr., "Where We Stand," *Wall Street Journal*, 27 September 1999, p. 5 (R).
15. Quoted in Pierson, *Tocqueville in America*, p. 244.

### The Perfectibility of Man

16. "The House That Jack Built," *Economist*, 18 September 1999: 23–26.
17. "How Jack Welch Runs GE," *Business Week*, 8 June 1998: 92–95.
18. Tocqueville, *Democracy in America*, vol. 2, p. 34.
19. Rich Morris, "The Others of Invention: Ig Nobels Honor the Tangentially Relevant," *Washington Post*, 2 October 1999, p. 1.
20. James P. Sterba, "Some Yanks Want a Shot at Playing British Aristocrats," *Wall Street Journal*, 20 October 1999, p. 1.
21. Barzini, *O America*, p. 404.

### A Tortured and Revolutionary People

22. See Seymour Martin Lipset, *American Exceptionalism* (New York: W. W. Norton, 1996), p. 21.
23. R. R. Palmer, *The Age of the Democratic Revolution*, vol. 1 (Princeton: Princeton University Press, 1959), pp. 189–90.
24. Tocqueville, *Democracy in America*, vol. 2, pp. 94 ff.

NOTES

25. David Hackett Fischer, *Albion's Seed: Four British Folkways in America* (New York and Oxford: Oxford University Press, 1989).
26. Tocqueville, *Democracy in America*, vol. 2, p. 136.
27. Barzini, *O America*, p. 273.
28. Ralph Barton Perry, *Characteristically American* (Freeport, N.Y.: Books for Libraries, 1949), p. 13.

### The Tyranny of the Majority

29. Jacques Maritain, *Reflections on America* (New York: Charles Scribner's Sons, 1958), p. 163.
30. Tocqueville, *Democracy in America* vol. 1, p. 255.
31. Ibid., p. 263.
32. Ibid., p. 264.
33. Tocqueville, *Democracy in America*, vol. 2, p. 11.
34. Ibid., p. 12.
35. Pierson, *Tocqueville in America*, p. 672.
36. Auberon Waugh, Preface to G. K. Chesterton, *The Complete Father Brown* (New York: Dodd, Mead, 1982), p. viii.

### CHAPTER 2:
### RELIGIOUS FAITH ANCHORED BY SECULAR INSTITUTIONS

1. Tocqueville, *Democracy in America*, vol. 1, p. 44.
2. Ibid., p. 308.
3. Cited in Lipset, *American Exceptionalism*, p. 61.
4. Kenneth D. Wald, *Religion and Politics in the United States* (New York: St. Martin's Press, 1987), pp. 6–7.

### A Uniquely Voluntary Religion

5. See Robert W. Fogel, "The Fourth Great Awakening and the Political Realignment of the 1990s," presented at the American Enterprise Institute, 27 April 1995.

6. Tocqueville, *Democracy in America*, vol. 1, p. 305.

7. "Fewer Find Faith in Church," *Detroit News*, 19 August 1999.

8. Michael Kahn, "Rent Rise Threatens to Silence Coltrane," *Washington Times*, 3 April 2000, p. 2.

9. Edmund Burke, *Collected Works* (Oxford, 1904), pp. 180–181. Cited in Lipset, *American Exceptionalism*, p. 60.

10. Tocqueville, *Democracy in America*, vol. 1, p. 306.

11. Ibid., p. 43.

12. Quoted in Barzini, *O America*, p. 235.

13. Christopher Lasch, *The Revolt of the Elites and the Betrayal of Democracy* (New York: W. W. Norton, 1995), p. 16.

14. Tocqueville, *Democracy in America*, vol. 2, p. 133.

15. Ibid., p. 22.

16. Tocqueville, *Democracy in America*, vol. 1, p. 43.

17. Ibid., p. 304.

18. Ibid., p. 305.

19. Michael Novak, *The Catholic Ethic and the Spirit of Capitalism* (New York: Free Press, 1993), p. 228.

### Church and State

20. Michael G. Kamen, *People of Paradox*: *An Inquiry Concerning the Origins of American Civilization* (New York: Vintage Books, 1973), p. 176.

21. William G. McLoughlin, "Pietism and the American Character," *American Quarterly* XVII (1965), p. 165.

22. Tocqueville, *Democracy in America*, vol. 1 p. 309.

23. Ibid., p. 143.

24. "Football Players Need a Hail Mary," *Washington Times*, 15 September 1999.

25. Tocqueville, *Democracy in America*, vol. 1, p. 306.

26. Benito Mussolini, for example, wrote a glowing review of Roosevelt's essays in 1934 in the official newspaper of the Italian Fascist regime, *Il Popolo d'Italia*.

27. Barzini, *O America*, p. 303.
28. Daniel Patrick Moynihan, *Counting Our Blessings* (Boston: Little, Brown, 1974), p. 177 ff.
29. Lorain Boettner, *Roman Catholicism* (Philadelphia: Presbyterian and Reformed Publishing Company, 1964), p. 3.
30. Dave Shiflett, "Holy and High Octane," *Wall Street Journal*, 24 September 1999, p. 21 (W).
31. Barzini, *O America*, p. 227.
32. Tocqueville, *Democracy in America*, vol. 2, p. 147.
33. Ibid., p. 150.

## CHAPTER 3:
## RUGGED INDIVIDUALISTS WITH A GENIUS FOR COOPERATION

1. Tocqueville, *Democracy in America*, vol. 2, p. 102.
2. Ibid., pp. 108–109.
3. Ibid., p. 103.
4. "Brotherhoods of Oddballs: America's Strange Clubs," *Economist*, U.S. Edition, 23 December 1995.
5. Tocqueville, *Democracy in America*, vol. 2, p. 107.
6. Ibid., p. 110.
7. Ibid., p. 171.
8. Ibid., p. 139.

### Families and Friends; Men and Women

9. Tocqueville, *Democracy in America*, vol. 2, p. 195.
10. Ibid., p. 196.
11. William H. McNeill, "Introductory Historical Commentary: The Fall of Great Power: Peace, Stability, and Legitimacy," Conference at Norske Nobelinstitutt, Oslo, Norway, June 1993, quoted in Lionel Tiger, *The Decline of Males* (New York: Golden Books 1999), p. 195.
12. Tocqueville, *Democracy in America*, vol. 2, p. 214.
13. Ibid., p. 203.

14. Ibid., p. 211.

14. Ibid., p. 211.
15. Ibid., p. 108.
16. Peter Drucker, *Managing in a Time of Great Change* (New York: Truman Talley Books/Plume 1998), p. 93.
17. Robert Bork, *Slouching Towards Gomorrah* (New York: Regan Books, 1996); Gertrude Himmelfarb, *The De-Moralization of Society: From Victorian Virtues to Modern Values* (New York: Alfred A. Knopf, 1994).
18. Tocqueville, *Democracy in America*, vol. 2, p. 119.
19. Tocqueville, *Democracy in America*, vol. 1, p. 187.
20. Tocqueville, *Democracy in America*, vol. 2, p. 184.

### Self-Interest, Rightly Understood

21. Tocqueville, *Democracy in America*, vol. 2, pp. 121–122.
22. Ibid., p. 122.
23. Ibid., p. 142.


## CHAPTER 4:
## ISOLATIONISTS CALLED TO INTERNATIONAL LEADERSHIP

1. Tocqueville, *Democracy in America*, vol. 1, p. 291.
2. David Laskin, "Land of the Free, Home of Bad Weather," *Wall Street Journal*, editorial page, 17 September 1999.
3. Barzini, *O America*, p. 158.
4. Tocqueville, *Democracy in America*, vol. 2, p. 101.
5. Barzini, *O America*, p. 303.
6. Tocqueville, *Democracy in America*, vol. 2, p. 268.
7. Tocqueville, *Democracy in America*, vol. 1, p. 203.
8. Ibid., p. 243.
9. Tocqueville, *Democracy in America*, vol. 2, p. 275.
10. Ibid., p. 278.
11. Ibid., p. 277.
12. Tocqueville, *Democracy in America*, vol. 1, p. 228.
13. Ibid., p. 235.

14. Ibid., p. 228.
15. Ibid., p. 235.
16. Ibid., p. 432.

### The Global Democratic Revolution

17. Tocqueville, *Democracy in America*, vol. 1, p. 434.
18. See Michael A. Ledeen, *Freedom Betrayed: How the United States Led a Global Democratic Revolution, Won the Cold War, and Walked Away* (Washington, D.C.: American Enterprise Institute, 1997).

### Contamination

19. Tocqueville, *Democracy in America*, vol. 2, p. 229.
20. Ibid., pp. 268–69.

## CHAPTER 5:
## APOSTLES OF FREEDOM TEMPTED BY LUXURIOUS TYRANNY

1. Tocqueville, *Democracy in America*, vol. 1, p. 260.
2. Tocqueville, *Democracy in America*, vol. 2, p. 288.
3. Ibid., p. 141.
4. Ibid., p. 320.
5. Ibid., p. 140 ff.
6. Ibid., p. 318.
7. Ibid., p. 319.
8. Ibid., p. 321.
9. Tocqueville *Democracy in America*, vol. 1, p. 227.
10. Cf. Jacob Talmon, *The Origins of Totalitarian Democracy* (New York: W. W. Norton, 1970, 1962).
11. Tocqueville, *Democracy in America*, vol. 2, p. 302.

### The Corruption of American Character

12. Tocqueville, *Democracy in America*, vol. 2, p. 141.
13. Ibid., p. 86.

14. "Voting Early and Often?" *Wall Street Journal*, 2 November 1999, p. 26 (A).
15. Tocqueville, *Democracy, in America*, vol. 2, p. 226.
16. Ibid., p. 227.

### Clinton: A New Form of Corruption

17. Michel Gurfinkiel, "The Sources of France's Corruption," *Wall Street Journal*, European edition, 3 November 1999.
18. Edward Timperlake and William Triplett, *Year of the Rat* (Washington, D.C.: Regnery, 1998).

### The Way Out

19. Tocqueville, *Democracy in America*, vol. 2, p. 296.
20. Tocqueville, *Democracy in America*, vol. 1, p. 318.
21. Ibid., p. 305.
22. Tocqueville, *Democracy in America*, vol. 2, p. 151.

## CONCLUSION:
## MORE TOCQUEVILLIAN THAN EVER BEFORE

1. DeVoto, *The Year of Decision: 1846*, p. 215.
2. Tocqueville, *Democracy in America*, vol. 2, p. 88.

# INDEX

# INDEX

# INDEX

# INDEX

225

# INDEX

# INDEX

# INDEX

# INDEX

survival options and the American
  character, 150
warfare and advancement, 148
warfare and freedom, 162
George Washington and the
  French Revolution, 153–54, 154–
  55
Tocqueville, Jules de, 18
Transparency International, 189
Triplett, Bill, 193
Trulock, Notra, 193
Truman, Harry, 33
Trump, Donald, 34
Turner, Frederick Jackson, 131
Turner, Ted, 86
Twain, Mark, 94

utopias (egalitarian), 82–83, 123

Vietnam War, 149
Voltaire, 44

*Wall Street Journal,* 39, 184
warfare, 142–44
  Cold War, 157–59, 183
  and freedom, 162–63
  intervention/isolationism, 141–42,
    153–54
  media coverage and, 152
  military achievement, 147–48
  military leaders, popularity of, 146–
    47
  military victory and the
    presidency, 33, 143
  patriotism, 144–45
  quick results, insistence on, 149
  Russia as America's archetypal
    opposite, 157–59
  survival options and the American
    character, 150

Vietnam War, 149
warfare and advancement, 148
World War I, 145–46
World War II, 146
  *See also* foreign policy
Washington, George, 33
  and the French Revolution, 153–
    54, 154–55
  as wartime leader turned president,
    143
*Washington Post,* 36
Waugh, Auberon, 67
wealth
  acquisition of, 58
  and equality of condition, 35–36
  philanthropy, 30, 85–86
  religion and material gain, 79–83
  social and economic mobility, 36–
    42
Weber, Max, 72, 80, 120
Welsh, "Neutron Jack," 43–44
Wesley, John, 80
Western Airlines, 42
Whitman, Walter, 66
Williams, Bill, 8
Wilson, Woodrow
  as wartime leader turned president,
    143
Winthrop, John, 51
Wolfe, Tom, 24
Wolsey, James, 69
Wolsey, Thomas, 69
women in America, 116–17
  character and physiology of, 15–16
  predominance in society, 118–19
Woolworth, 42
World War I, 145–46, 157
World War II, 146, 157

Young, Andrew, 78